# Lecture Notes in Computer Science

# Lecture Notes in Computer Science

# Lecture Notes in Computer Science

Edited by G. Goos and J. Hartmanis

## 260

David C. Luckham
Friedrich W. von Henke
Bernd Krieg-Brückner
Olaf Owe

# ANNA
# A Language for
# Annotating Ada Programs

Reference Manual

Springer-Verlag

Berlin Heidelberg New York London Paris Tokyo

**Authors**

David C. Luckham
Computer Systems Laboratory, Stanford University
Stanford, CA 94305-2192, USA

Friedrich W. von Henke
SRI International
333 Ravenswood Avenue, Menlo Park, CA 94025, USA

Bernd Krieg-Brückner
FB 3 Mathematik-Informatik, Universität Bremen
Postfach 330 440, 2800 Bremen 33
Federal Republic of Germany

Olaf Owe
Institute of Informatics, University of Oslo
P.O. Box 1080, Blindern, 0316 Oslo 3, Norway

CR Subject Classification (1987): D.2.1, D.2.2, D.2.4, D.2.5, D.2.10, D.3.2, I.2.2, I.2.4

ISBN 3-540-17980-1 Springer-Verlag Berlin Heidelberg New York
ISBN 0-387-17980-1 Springer-Verlag New York Berlin Heidelberg

Library of Congress Cataloging-in-Publication Data. ANNA, a language for annotating Ada programs. (Lecture notes in computer science; 260) Bibliography: p. Includes index. 1. ANNA (Computer program language) 2. Ada (Computer program language) I. Luckham, David C. II. Title: ANNA. III. Series. QA76.73.A54A56 1987 005.13 87-13030 ISBN 0-387-17980-1 (U.S.)

© Springer-Verlag Berlin Heidelberg 1987
Printed in Germany

Printing and binding: Druckhaus Beltz, Hemsbach/Bergstr.
2145/3140-543210

# Table of Contents

# PREFACE

Anna is a language extension of Ada to include facilities for formally specifying the intended behavior of Ada programs. It is designed to meet a perceived need to augment Ada with precise machine-processable annotations so that well established formal methods of specification and documentation can be applied to Ada programs.

The current Anna design includes annotations of all Ada constructs except tasking. Similar extensions for formal specification can be made to other Algol-like languages such as Pascal, PL-1, Concurrent Pascal, and Modula; essentially, these extensions would be subsets of Anna.

The design of Anna was initiated in 1980 by Bernd Krieg-Brueckner and David Luckham. An outline of some of the main features of Anna was presented at the Ada Symposium held in Boston, December 1980 [12]. This was based on the preliminary Ada design [11]. The current Anna design is a significant development from the 1980 version and was undertaken by the four present authors over the period 1981 — 1984. This effort proceeded in parallel with the Ada language revisions. It was sponsored by the Defense Advanced Research Projects Agency as part of the research project of the Program Analysis and Verification Group at Stanford University. The current Anna design corresponds to the latest Ada design. ANSI/MIL-STD 1815A.

### Design Goals
The design of Anna was undertaken from the beginning with four principal considerations:

1. Constructing annotations should be easy for the Ada programmer and should depend as much as possible on notation and concepts of Ada.

2. Anna should possess language features that are widely used in the specification and documentation of programs.

3. Anna should provide a framework within which the various established theories of formally specifying programs may be applied to Ada.

4. Annotations should be equally well suited for different possible applications during the life cycle of a program. Such applications include not only testing, debugging and formal verification of a finished program, but also specification of program parts during the earlier stages of requirements analysis and program design.

### Adaption to Ada
Goal (1) has had a major influence on both the syntax and semantics of Anna. The Anna syntax is a straightforward extension of the Ada syntax. Formal comments occur within the Ada comment framework. Anna programs are therefore accepted by Ada compilers. Ada concepts such as scope and visibility, elaboration, and generic instantiation apply to annotations. Most new concepts in Anna are extensions of concepts in Ada. For example Boolean expressions are extended to allow quantification. Collections of designated values associated with access types are available in annotations using the attribute notation of Ada. The central specification concept in Anna, the declarative annotation, is a generalization of the constraint concept in Ada and obeys the same Ada scope rules.

## Basic Specification Techniques

Goal (2) requires that the underlying annotation language should be at least as powerful as any first order logic; i.e., it should contain the syntactic category of Ada expressions extended by logical quantifiers and implication operators. This choice is clearly dictated by the fact that most comments (informal or formal) are Boolean relationships between program variables. Also, in practice, annotations will often contain partially defined expressions, so the semantics of Anna must define clearly the meaning of such annotations.

Previous studies in program specification also indicate that inclusion of Ada text as formal comments — called virtual Ada text — should be permitted in Anna. This provides a powerful method of constructing executable specifications and syntactically separating them from the subject text.

Based on these decisions, the simplest kinds of annotations in Anna permit previous techniques for specifying Pascal programs to be applied to Ada [7, 10, 15, 17].

## Established Specification Methods

Goal (3) is concerned with providing facilities for applying various established specification techniques that go beyond the simple comment or assertional techniques. For example, the most successful method of specifying access variable manipulations requires that annotations may refer to objects that are not available in the programming language, i.e., Collections [15]. (See also [Ada83 3.8 (3)].) Therefore access type collections and standard operations on them are provided in Anna as predefined attributes. Similarly, techniques for specifying module constructs by means of sequences of operations have been developed in previous literature, e.g., [16, 4] and [13]. Facilities for specifying packages in Anna include package states and sequences of state transitions. These facilities, together with the package axiom annotation, also enable the Anna user to apply other specification methods, e.g., the various algebraic methods of specifying abstract data types [8, 5], to packages.

To allow the specification of programs that may raise or propagate exceptions, propagation annotations are included in a notation adapted to Ada from [14].

## Applications of Formal Annotations

Goal (4) is concerned with developing new applications of formal annotations. Use of Anna is not intended to be restricted to only verification of existing programs in the conventional proof-theoretic sense although this is clearly a major possible future application. A significant part of this document is devoted to describing a method of transforming annotations into runtime checks. It is applicable to most kinds of annotations. Consequently, an Anna program (or, in the most general case, large parts of an Anna program) can be transformed into an Ada program with runtime checks for consistency with the original annotations. This method can be implemented more easily than a formal verification system, and will provide a useful tool for testing and debugging Ada programs.

Anna is also intended for use during the design of a program, e.g., for formal specification of subprograms and packages prior to implementation of their bodies. Anna specifications may be generated as part of the development process from earlier requirements [3], and may then accompany a program through all stages of its development. (See also [2].)

## Future Versions of Anna

Our philosophy in the current Anna design has been to provide a minimal set of basic kinds of annotations and predefined annotation concepts. It is the user's responsibility to define the special concepts needed for an application. As experience with Ada specifications and annotations accumulates we expect to revise and expand future versions.

It is certainly true that some features of Ada make it difficult to design an adequate annotation language. Any attempt to provide for every possibility, or to overly generalize facilities, will lead to a very complicated design.

The problems are caused to some extent by the basic set of Ada constructs, for example, access types and tasking. Specification of access type manipulations has always been a problem in previous languages such as Pascal, and one wishes that high level languages would progress to a stage where access types were omitted. Previous facilities appear to be the bare minimum for specification but do not seem to make the job easy in any real sense. The current facilities in Anna for specifying access type manipulations in particular, and composite types in general, may be extended in future versions.

Anna does not include any specific annotations for tasking. Some annotation can be provided for tasks by means of the facilities for subprograms. In general we feel that research in the overall area of specification of concurrent computation needs to progress before we make any extensions to Anna for tasking.

Most complications in the Anna design, however, are caused by the generality and permissiveness of Ada visibility rules, naming, overloading, and elaboration. In some cases the complicated Ada rules spill over into Anna; this we cannot avoid. In others, e.g., packages, the specialized annotations will not be useful if the programmer uses Ada in the wildest possible ways. Certainly, part of useful annotation is disciplined use of Ada; this matter will be addressed in one of the forthcoming Anna documents.

Anna can be modified for use as a program design language (PDL) at early stages of the software development process. This possibility is being studied and seems to improve on existing PDLs. It would provide automated analysis for some kinds of design errors during early systems design phases.

## Documents and Support Tools

The preliminary reference manual is the first of a number of documents and planned support tools for Anna. Documents in preparation include: (1) An introduction to the use of Anna. This will include examples of various applications of formal annotations and a rationale for certain parts of the design. (2) Transformations from annotations to Ada runtime checks. (3) An axiomatic semantics of Anna.

Anna support tools currently being developed include : (1) syntax analyzers, structured editors, and tools for detecting simple kinds of errors; (2) a runtime checking system that will translate most annotations into Ada runtime checks. Development of this system as part of an environment of tools for debugging and testing by directly executing an Ada program against its Anna specifications is planned. A formal verification system is regarded as a longer-term undertaking.

## Acknowledgements

Numerous comments on the November 1982 version of the preliminary Anna manual have been helpful in revising the design and producing this present manual. We owe special thanks to Norman Cohen, Anthony Gargaro, and Alec D. Hill for detailed reviews of that document which were most helpful. We are also greatly indebted to Rosemary Brock for her consistent efforts in preparing the manuscripts of the various versions of this manual over the past two years.

## Acknowledgement to the first revision

This revision incorporates many of the corrections and suggestions over the past two years arising from the use of Anna and from the implementation of tools to support its applications. Our thanks are due to Doug Bryan, Chris Byrnes, Rob Chang, Geoff Mendal, Randall Neff, David Rosenblum, Sriram Sankar, and Will Tracz. As before, we are again indebted to Rosemary for overseeing the manuscript.

This work was supported by the Advanced Research Projects Agency, Department of Defense, under contracts N00039-82-C-0250 and N00039-84-C-0211.

# 1. BASIC ANNA CONCEPTS

Anna is an extension of Ada. An Anna program consists of an Ada program which has been augmented by formal comments. Anna defines two kinds of formal comments, which are introduced by special comment indicators in order to distinguish them from informal comments: *virtual Ada text*, and *annotations*. In an Anna program, formal comments must satisfy the lexical, syntactic and semantic rules of Anna.

We refer to the Ada part of an Anna program as the *underlying Ada program*. Formal comments are comments in the underlying Ada program.


## 1.1 VIRTUAL ADA TEXT

A comment starting with the indicator consisting of a double hyphen followed by a colon, `--:`, is called *virtual Ada text*. In contrast, parts of the underlying Ada program are called *actual Ada text*.

The purpose of virtual Ada text is to define concepts used in annotations. Concepts may be defined in virtual declarations of additional objects, types, subprograms, and packages. Virtual text may also be used to compute values that are needed in annotations but are not available in the underlying program.

Virtual text is Ada text. Virtual text may be one of the following: a virtual basic declaration, a virtual body, a virtual statement, a virtual compilation unit, a virtual with clause, a virtual use clause, or a virtual exception handler. With the exceptions listed below, virtual text must obey the lexical, syntactic, and semantic rules of Ada and must be legal in the context of the underlying Ada program. This means that for virtual text to be legal it must be legal Ada if the formal comment indicators preceding it are removed. Consequently, a virtual declaration may appear only in a (virtual or actual) declarative part etc., and virtual text must obey the Ada visibility rules.

Virtual text may not syntactically contain actual Ada text; for example, it is not permitted to enclose actual Ada statements in a virtual block.

Virtual text may refer to any entity declared in the underlying program (the actual Ada text), in accordance with the Ada visibility rules. However, virtual text may not include any text whose elaboration or execution might change actual Ada objects. Thus the following are excluded from virtual text: any virtual declaration that would hide an actual declaration, any assignment to an actual object, any subprogram call with an actual variable as **in out** or **out** parameter, any call to a subprogram that might change an actual variable global to the subprogram, and any allocator for an actual access type.

Moreover, the execution of a virtual text may not change the flow of control of the underlying program. Thus virtual **return**, **exit**, and **goto** statements may only appear in a virtual block or body and may not transfer control out of the largest enclosing virtual block or body. The same restriction applies to virtual raise statements except for raising the predefined exception, ANNA_ERROR. Also, a virtual exception handler within the handlers for an actual block or body is only allowed for ANNA_ERROR.

Any entity declared in virtual text (i.e., virtual declarations) may only be referred to in formal comments; it is not accessible from the underlying Ada program.

The only exceptions to the applicability of Ada rules to virtual text are the following:

1. Bodies of virtual subprograms and private parts and bodies of virtual packages need not be supplied (see 3.9).

2. The Anna membership test is in (see 4.5.2), the Anna predefined equality on limited types, the additional Anna attributes, and entities in the Anna environment (see Appendix C) may be used in virtual text.

Virtual Ada text may be annotated like the underlying Ada text.

*Example of a virtual variable and a virtual function:*

```
--: GHOST : INTEGER;
--: function LENGTH return NATURAL;
--   GHOST and LENGTH may only be referred to in formal comments.
```

*Example of a virtual type definition using an actual type:*

```
    type ITEM is ...;

--: type HISTORY_SEQUENCE;
--: type PTR is access HISTORY_SEQUENCE;
--: type HISTORY_SEQUENCE is
--:      record
--:           DATA : ITEM;
--:           NEXT : PTR;
--:      end record;
```

*Notes:*

The legality rules that restrict virtual text are such that conformance with them can be checked in an Anna implementation; this requires only straightforward extensions to Ada parsing and static semantic analysis.

These rules exclude the obvious cases where virtual text might change the behavior of the underlying Ada program if it is executed together with the actual Ada text. However, the legality rules are not strong enough to exclude all such cases. For example, a call to a virtual subprogram may fail to terminate.

Virtual exception handlers for virtual blocks and bodies may handle any exception, actual or virtual.

The rules for virtual text disallow calls to a subprogram with side effects on actual objects. This also disallows virtual calls to subprograms of an actual package that change the package state (see 3.2, 7.7).

## 1.2 ANNOTATIONS

A comment starting with the indicator consisting of a double hyphen followed by a vertical bar (or exclamation mark), `--|`, is called an *annotation*. Anna defines lexical, syntactic and semantic rules that must be satisfied by annotations. Most annotations involve Anna expressions, which extend the category of Ada expressions. The meaning of annotations is indicated by their syntactic form and their position.

Annotations use two kinds of variables: *logical variables* and *program variables*. A variable may be declared by a quantifier (see 4.11) or in special forms of annotations (subtype annotations, see 3.3, or result annotations, see 6.5); such a variable is called a *logical variable*. A component of a logical variable of composite type is also a logical variable. The scope of a logical variable is the text from the first occurrence of the variable (its declaration) to the end of the quantified expression or annotation in which it is declared (see also 8.2 and 8.3).

A variable that is not a logical variable in an annotation must be a *program variable*, i.e., a variable visible in the (actual or virtual) Ada text at the point where the annotation appears.

The notion of a program variable corresponds to the Ada notion of variable (i.e., non-constant object); it includes component names and slices, objects designated by access values and formal in out and out parameters of subprograms. A program variable may also appear in the name of another variable; for example, in the annotation

```
--| A(K) > J;
```

K is a program variable that is also part of the name of the variable (indexed component) A(K). In addition, certain components of computation states whose values can be named explicitly in Anna (collections, see 3.8, and package states, see 7.7) are treated in annotations like program variables. The program variables occurring in an annotation are sometimes referred to as its *constituent program variables*.

Ada semantics prescribes that the value of a program variable is undefined before initialization. Anna provides a boolean-valued attribute DEFINED to express whether or not the value of a variable is defined: For a scalar variable V, V'DEFINED expresses whether V has been initialized (see 3.5); for a composite variable A, A'DEFINED expresses whether the values of all components of A are fully defined (see 3.6, 3.7).

Annotations may be part of a generic unit and are instantiated according to the Ada rules (see 12.2).

An annotation has a scope of application that is a region of program text for which it has a meaning. The scope of an annotation is determined according to the Ada scope rules from its position in the text.

An annotation is elaborated at the place in the text where it appears. In general, elaboration of an annotation involves evaluating variables and expressions whose initial values are required in the annotation (see 4.13). Specific rules for elaboration are given in the sections on individual kinds of annotations.

Anna annotations generalize the Ada concept of constraint; they constrain the values of program variables. The scope and kind of an annotation determines where the constraint must hold. The general concepts used in defining the meaning of annotations are discussed in the following sections. Legal positions of formal comments are described in Chapter 2; syntax and informal semantics of specific kinds of annotations in Anna are given in Chapters 3 to 13 of this document.

Elaboration, instantiation and evaluation of annotations must not have any effect on the values of actual or virtual program variables. As a consequence, calls to functions with side effects and allocators are excluded from annotations.

Elaboration, instantiation, and evaluation of an annotation also must not depend on the values of any actual or virtual program variables other than its constituent variables. Consequently, the value of an annotation can change only if one of its constituent variables changes value.

*Examples of annotations:*

```
    MAX   :   INTEGER;
--|  0 ≤ MAX ≤ 100;
--    MAX is a program variable constrained by the annotation (see 3.2).
--    The values of MAX must satisfy the annotation throughout its scope.

    subtype EVEN is INTEGER;
--|       where X : EVEN => X mod 2 = 0;
--    All values of subtype EVEN must be divisible by 2. X is a logical variable.
--    Note that this annotation cannot be expressed as an Ada constraint.

    function IS_EVEN(Y : INTEGER) return BOOLEAN;
--|       where return Y isin EVEN;
--    The values returned by IS_EVEN must satisfy the constraint on the subtype, EVEN.
--    Y is a program variable in the annotation and is evaluated at each call to IS_EVEN.

    function IS_PRIME(P : NATURAL) return BOOLEAN;
--|       where
--|          return not exist X,Y : NATURAL =>
--|              X > 1 and Y > 1 and X*Y = P;
--    The result annotation defining primeness constrains the values returned by
--    IS_PRIME. X and Y are logical variables declared by the quantifier exist;
--    P is a program variable.
```

## 1.3 SEMANTICS OF ANNOTATIONS

### 1.3.1 Program States

The semantics of annotations are defined in terms of *program states*. A program state gives the association of values with the program variables at a particular point in a computation. The Anna concept of *state* — or, for emphasis, *observable state* — is derived from the Ada concept of a *simple statement* as the elementary unit of observable action; the smallest observable state transition is the execution of a simple statement or the elaboration of a declaration. An annotation constrains the observable states that occur during elaboration and execution in the scope of the annotation. The set of states associated with the scope of an annotation includes the *initial state*, which is the state in which the annotation is elaborated. The set of states associated with the scope is generated from the initial state by elaborating the declarations (if any) and then executing the simple statements in the scope. For emphasis, we refer to the simple statements in a compound statement or body as the *constituent simple statements*.

The *final state* in the execution of a scope is the state reached on *normal termination*, i.e. when normal execution of the statements in the scope is completed (cf. [Ada83, 9.4]); this includes the cases where execution of the scope is completed by executing a return statement or an exit statement, or where the scope is left by executing a goto statement. The final state is *not* reached if execution of the scope is completed by propagating an exception (it is then said to *terminate exceptionally*) or does not terminate at all.

Note that the set of states associated with a scope does not include intermediate states that occur during elaboration of one declaration or execution of a constituent simple statement, for example during execution of a subprogram call.

### 1.3.2 Assertions and the Anna Kernel

An annotation that constrains only one state is called an *assertion*. In Anna, all annotations have a scope, and thus constrain possibly more than one state. However, an assertion can be expressed in Anna by a simple statement annotation (see 5.1), or by an object annotation that constrains only one state (the initial or final state) in its scope (i.e. an in or out annotation, see 3.2).

The assertion is the fundamental concept in terms of which the meaning of most of the remainder of Anna is defined. The semantics of annotations are defined by means of a *transformation* which reduces Anna text to an *Anna Kernel*. The Anna Kernel is a subset of Anna in which most annotations are assertions; the only annotations not reduced to assertions (and thus remaining in the Kernel) are axiomatic annotations (see 7.8), context annotations (see 10.1.3), constraints on function results (i.e., result annotations (see 6.5)) and some constraints that result from subtype annotations (see 3.3): on the result of Ada membership tests (see 4.5.2), type conversions and qualified expressions. The rules for the transformation into the Anna Kernel describe how different kinds of annotations are transformed into sets of assertions and virtual Ada text. The transformation rules are explained informally for each kind of annotation in the relevant section of this document.

### 1.3.3 Consistency of Anna Programs

An Anna program is called *consistent* if all Ada text (including both actual and virtual text) is consistent with the annotations, and execution of the virtual Ada text does not change the behavior of the actual underlying Ada text. The semantics of most annotations are expressed as constraints on program states. Ada text is consistent with such annotations if all computation states satisfy the constraints imposed by the annotations. Consistency of an Anna program is equivalent to consistency of the corresponding Anna Kernel program, that is *if all assertions generated by transforming the annotations are true in the states to which they apply.*

Consistency of Ada text with annotations that are not reduced to assertions in the Kernel is defined directly. Ada text is consistent with constraints on function results if all function calls return values consistent with the result annotations on the functions (see 6.5), and consistent with constraints on Ada membership tests, type conversions and qualified expressions if all Ada membership tests, type conversions and qualified expressions yield values that are consistent with constraints on the types involved (see 3.3, 4.5.2, 4.6, 4.7). Axiomatic annotations constrain the implementation of a package; consistency between axiomatic annotations and package bodies is defined in Section 7.9. Context annotations restrict the global variables that can be referenced in a program unit; see 10.1.3 for the definition of their semantics.

Since not all virtual subprograms and packages may have bodies, consistency is relative to the assumption that for virtual program units without bodies one could supply bodies which satisfy the annotations of their declarations.

For the purpose of formally analyzing consistency of Anna programs, the meaning of a program in the Anna Kernel (containing virtual Ada text, assertions and those annotations that do not get reduced to assertions, in addition to the underlying Ada program) is defined by a system of axioms and proof rules. This system is based on the logic of programs originally introduced by Hoare [7]. The logic formalizes consistency of Ada text with assertions. It is commonly called a "weak" logic. A proof of consistency in the weak logic implies that any state reached during a computation will satisfy the constraints of any annotation that applies to that state. A proof in this logic does not imply that a state to which an assertion applies is ever reached in an actual computation. In particular, proofs in the weak logic do not imply termination of computations. If it is required to establish that a program actually reaches a particular state (or terminates), other techniques must be used.

The axiomatic system for Anna extends the traditional logic of programs by permitting assertions themselves to be undefined for certain values of the program variables (see below). In this document we rely on an intuitive understanding of the meaning of assertions. An alternative method of consistency analysis by checking the truth of assertions at runtime is outlined in Section 1.4.

*Notes:*

Some constraints (for instance, most range constraints) can be expressed either as an Ada constraint or as an Anna annotation. If such a constraint is satisfied (in either form) it does not matter in which form it is expressed; otherwise the behavior of the underlying Ada program will depend on whether the constraint is part of the actual Ada text or not.

The legality rules for virtual Ada text imply that execution of virtual text can result in a change in the behavior of the actual Ada program only if an exception is propagated out of virtual Ada text.

### 1.3.4 Definedness of Annotations

Annotations are written in a modified form of first-order logic in which functions and predicates may be partially defined. A boolean expression in an annotation or assertion may not have a defined value in a given state because its evaluation does not terminate or propagates an exception (see 4.14 for a precise definition of definedness of expressions).

If an annotation (or an assertion generated from it) has an undefined value for a state in a computation then it is not satisfied by that computation, and it is considered to be inconsistent with the surrounding Ada text. Consequently, when an annotation has an undefined value in a state, the effect is the same as if it was false in that state; the Anna program in which the annotation occurs is regarded as inconsistent.

## 1.4 CONSISTENCY CHECKING

For most Anna programs it is possible to check the consistency of the underlying Ada text with its annotations during execution of the program. Checking is an alternative form of consistency analysis which complements formal methods of consistency proof; it is not as powerful as a formal proof but can be implemented as an extension of an Ada compiler. In this document, one particular method of consistency checking is presented: we refer to it as *the checking method*.

The checking method, like the axiomatic proof method, is based on the transformation of an Anna program into an Anna Kernel program as mentioned in Section 1.3. The checking method is therefore only concerned with checking the assertions that result from transforming annotations. Since an assertion is required to be true only in a particular state, its truth can be checked at runtime by executing extra (virtual) Ada code which evaluates the assertion in that state.

For the purpose of checking, an assertion

```
--| boolean_expression;
```

is translated into the following virtual Ada text:

```
--: begin
--:     if not (boolean_expression) then
--:         ...                              --  report inconsistency
--:             raise ANNA_ERROR;
--:         end if;
--: exception
--:     when ANNA_ERROR =>
--:             raise ANNA_ERROR;
--:     when others =>
--:         ...                              --  report exception during checking
--:             raise ANNA_ERROR;
--: end;
```

This basic translation scheme needs to be extended if the boolean expression contains quantifiers, conditional expressions, Anna membership tests, or other expressions that are legal in Anna but not in Ada.

The result of translating all assertions accordingly is an Ada program that consists of the actual Ada text, the virtual text of the original Anna program, and the newly generated (virtual) checking code; execution of this augmented program will perform runtime checks of all assertions. If the execution terminates without the exception ANNA_ERROR, which is predefined in Anna, ever being raised, and no exception is propagated out of virtual text, then the underlying Ada program is consistent with the virtual Ada text and the annotations for that particular set of inputs.

The behavior of the underlying Ada program is not changed by the execution of the checking code if no inconsistency is found. If checking does not terminate in a given amount of time, the Ada program may still be provable to be consistent with the annotations.

If an inconsistency is detected, checking will raise the exception ANNA_ERROR and report the inconsistency; the execution of the Ada program will then be aborted, unless the user has provided for special handling of the exceptions raised by the checking code or an others handler exists. The purpose of (re)raising the exception ANNA_ERROR is to allow the user of an Anna checker to do specialized error recovery by including exception handlers for ANNA_ERROR in virtual Ada text. However, the effect of executing such an Anna program with checking is not guaranteed to be the same as that of executing the underlying Ada program if the checked Anna program terminates and an inconsistency or exception has been reported during checking.

Consistency checking is possible for most of Anna, including quantified expressions; it does not include checking of consistency between package axioms and package bodies (see Chapter 7), and for annotations involving virtual functions for which a body or definite return expression has not been provided (see 6.5). The translation of different kinds of annotations into assertions and associated checking code is described informally in the relevant sections of this document.

## 1.5 STRUCTURE OF THE MANUAL

The main body of this manual is structured in the same way as the Ada Programming Language Reference Manual [1]. It should be read as an extension to that document, informally describing the lexical elements, syntax and semantics of Anna. References to the Ada Manual are given in the format [Ada83, Chapter.Section].

Each section is devoted either to describing a particular kind of annotation or to explaining a basic concept such as definedness or consistency. Those sections describing a particular kind of annotation are organized as follows: description of syntax, elaboration, semantics (i.e., an informal description of the meaning of the annotation), and the transformation of the annotation into Anna Kernel text. Examples and notes follow as usual. Note that the transformation provides a complementary description of the semantics of an annotation.

The syntax of Anna is an extension of the context-free syntax of Ada. The syntax rules of Anna denote new syntactic categories or else replacements for rules in Ada with the same name. An Anna rule is often obtained from an Ada rule either by additional clauses or by extension of the clauses in the Ada rule. In these cases a reference to the Ada rule enclosed by three dots is placed on the right side of the Anna rule. Thus, an example of additional clauses,

```
name ::=
    ... ada_name ...
  | initial_name
  | state
```

indicates that Anna names are the set of Ada names extended by the new categories for initial names and states. The Anna rule is obtained by adding the new alternative clauses to the right side of the Ada rule. Similarly, an example of an Anna rule obtained by extending the clauses of an Ada rule is,

```
compound_statement ::=
    [with
        basic_annotation  {, basic_annotation} ;]
    ... ada_compound_statement ...
```

The clauses in the Anna compound statement rule are the clauses of the Ada rule, each preceded by an optional annotation starting with the reserved word **with**.

As in the syntax for Ada, italic prefixes to the nonterminals, e.g. *"boolean_"*, are intended to convey semantic information; such nonterminals are syntactically equivalent to the unprefixed category. Only new or modified syntax rules are listed in this manual.

The Anna syntax includes two kinds of rules that modify an Ada syntactic category. The first kind defines the legal position of a particular kind of annotation within (actual or virtual) Ada text; the rule given above for compound statements is an example. Annotation text may not be included at any place an Ada comment may appear; its inclusion is restricted just like inclusion of virtual text (see 1.1): an annotation may appear in Ada text only in the form and in the position defined by such a rule.

The second kind of rule extends an Ada syntactic category, like the rule for names above. These rules apply only to annotations and not to (actual or virtual) Ada text, the syntax of which remains unchanged.

The separation of virtual Ada text and annotations from the underlying Ada program by formal comment indicators is not represented in the syntax of Anna, but is nevertheless lexically enforced to make every legal Anna program a legal Ada program.

Throughout this manual, examples of Anna text are supposed to be consistent unless explicitly stated otherwise.

*Note*: Square brackets in states are terminal symbols, indicated by boldface "**[ ]**".

## 1.6 CLASSIFICATION OF ERRORS

In Anna programs, there are the following additional categories of errors:

1. Errors that must be detected at compilation time by every Anna compiler. These errors are analogous to error category (a) for Ada.

2. Inconsistent Anna program errors. Inconsistency may be detected either by attempting a proof using proof rules (see 1.3.3) or by the checking method (see 1.4) at runtime.

# 2. LEXICAL ELEMENTS

The lexical elements and conventions of Anna are those of Ada, with the extensions described in this chapter.

## 2.1 CHARACTER SET

On some equipment concise graphic characters are available to denote conventional mathematical symbols. These Anna special characters may be used in annotations to improve readability, but need not be supported by an Anna implementation.

```
graphic_character ::=
    ... ada_graphic_character ...
  | anna_special_character
```

Rules for replacement with characters from the basic character set are given in Section 2.10.

The following additional characters may be used in an annotation:

(g) Anna special characters

$$\neg \quad \wedge \quad \vee \quad \rightarrow \quad \leftrightarrow \quad \exists \quad \forall \quad \neq \quad \leq \quad \geq$$

*Notes:*

The following names are used when referring to Anna special charcters:

| Symbol | Name | Symbol | Name |
|--------|------|--------|------|
| $\neg$ | not | $\forall$ | for all |
| $\wedge$ | and | $\exists$ | there exists |
| $\vee$ | or | $\neq$ | not equal |
| $\rightarrow$ | implies | $\leq$ | less or equal |
| $\leftrightarrow$ | if and only if | $\geq$ | greater or equal |

## 2.2 LEXICAL ELEMENTS, SEPARATORS, AND DELIMITERS

The following additional compound delimiters may be used in annotations:

$$\text{->} \qquad \text{<->} \qquad \text{(\textbackslash} \qquad \text{\textbackslash)}$$

**2.3 - 2.6**          No additions


## 2.7 FORMAL COMMENTS

Anna permits two kinds of formal comments, which start with special formal comment indicators: virtual Ada text starting with `--:`, and annotations starting with `--|` or `--!`.

The legal position of formal comments is restricted by the syntax of Anna. Formal comments may not appear in an Anna program everywhere an Ada comment may appear. For example, an Ada expression may be broken up by an Ada comment, but not by virtual text or an annotation. Virtual Ada text may appear only where it would be legal in Ada if the comment indicators preceding it were removed (see 1.1). Similarly, a declarative annotation may only appear in an Ada declarative part, and a statement annotation only in a statement position. For each kind of annotation, the syntax of Anna specifies in what position it may appear (see 1.5).

The syntactic description of Anna omits the formal comment indicators `--:` and `--|`, it being understood that each line of an Anna formal comment must start with one of these indicators. Thus a formal comment that runs over several lines must start with a new comment indicator on each continuation line. On the other hand, more than one annotation may appear in one line of formal comment text.

*Example of an annotation extending over more than one line:*

```
     function DEFINED(S : STRING) return BOOLEAN;
--|       where return exist I : INDEX_RANGE =>
--|            TABLE(I).MEMBER = S and TABLE(I).LEVEL = LEXLEVEL;
```


**2.8**          No additions


## 2.9 RESERVED WORDS

The following additional words are reserved in annotations (but not in Ada text):

axiom          exist          isin          to          where

## 2.10 ALLOWED REPLACEMENTS OF CHARACTERS

The following additional replacements are allowed in annotations:

| | |
|---|---|
| \| | ! |
| [ | (\ |
| ] | \) |
| ¬ | not |
| ∧ | and |
| ∨ | or |
| → | -> |
| ↔ | <-> |
| ∃ | exist |
| ∀ | for all |
| ≠ | /= |
| ≤ | <= |
| ≥ | >= |

# 3. ANNOTATIONS OF DECLARATIONS AND TYPES

In this chapter we describe annotations on object, type and subtype declarations.

The general concepts for annotations on objects are described in Section 3.2. Special operations for annotating scalar objects are described in Section 3.5; special operations and concepts for annotating composite objects are described in Sections 3.6-3.8. The special facilities for composite objects include the *collection* attribute of an access type, and new primary terms representing the *state* of an array, record or collection. The notation for states of arrays, records and collections is based on sequences of operations and is a special case of the notation for package states introduced in Chapter 7. Anna treats objects of composite types as special cases of the package concept.

The use of array, record, and collection states to annotate programs (originally Pascal programs) has been described in [15]. These techniques may be applied directly to Ada programs by means of Anna composite type facilities. We note that [Ada83, 3.8] refers to *Collections*: "The objects designated by the values of an access type form a *collection* implicitly associated with the type." In Anna the collection is introduced explicitly for annotation.

## 3.1 DECLARATIVE ANNOTATIONS

Declarative annotations are annotations placed in a declarative part or in a package specification. Declarative annotations generalize the Ada concept of type constraint in two ways: (1) they may impose more general restrictions on values than those expressible by Ada constraints, and (2) they may be applied to entities other than types and objects.

```
basic_declaration ::=
        ... ada_basic_declaration ...
    | basic_annotation_list
    | axiomatic_annotation
    | state_type_annotation

basic_annotation_list ::=
        basic_annotation  {, basic_annotation};

basic_annotation ::=
        object_annotation
    | result_annotation
    | propagation_annotation
```

Annotations that either appear in the position of a declaration (i.e. basic annotations and axiomatic annotations) or are syntactically tied to a declaration by the reserved word **where** (subtype annotations, see 3.3, and subprogram annotations, see 6.1) are collectively called *declarative annotations*. The scope of a declarative annotation is the same as for an Ada declaration at that position. A declarative annotation is elaborated at the point where it occurs (following the Ada rules of linear elaboration), except for subprogram annotations (see 6.1).

In general, the meaning of a declarative annotation is that it defines a restriction on certain values computed within its scope. The precise meaning of each kind of declarative annotation is explained in the section dealing with that kind of annotation. The meaning of a list of basic annotations (separated by ",") is the same as that of a sequence of basic annotations (separated by ";"); in either case, the restrictions or constraints expressed by all individual basic annotations must be satisfied. (For an explanation of the difference between lists or sequences of annotations and conjunctions of annotations see 3.2.)

*Example of an Anna object annotation expressing a condition analogous to an Ada constraint:*

```
    INDEX : INTEGER; --| 0 ≤ INDEX ≤ in SIZE;
--    corresponds to the Ada declaration INDEX : INTEGER range 0 .. SIZE;
```

*Example of an Anna subtype annotation not expressible by an Ada constraint:*

```
    subtype ODD_PRIME is INTEGER;
--|       where X : ODD_PRIME => X mod 2 = 1 and IS_PRIME(X);
--        IS_PRIME is a previously declared boolean-valued function (see 1.2).
```

*Example of a subprogram annotation (see Chapter 6):*

```
    procedure SWAP(U, V : in out ELEM);
--|       where out (U = in V and V = in U);
```

*Notes:*

A declarative annotation is not considered a part of any preceding Ada declaration, even when it is bound to a preceding declaration by the reserved word **where** (see 3.3, 6.1); thus all identifiers declared in preceding declarations are visible in a declarative annotation (see 8.3).

A declarative object annotation must occur in the position of a basic declaration.


## 3.2 ANNOTATIONS OF OBJECTS

An object is an entity that has a value of a given type. In Anna, objects are the Ada objects [Ada83, 3.2], the collections associated with access types (see 3.8.4), and the states of nongeneric packages (see 7.7). In Anna, the words '*object*' and '*variable*' always refer to this more general class of entities.

A declarative annotation on objects is a boolean-valued compound expression appearing in a declarative part. Within the scope of the annotation, the annotation constrains the values of the objects that occur in the expression as program variables.

```
object_annotation ::=
        boolean_compound_expression
      | out boolean_primary
```

Three kinds of object annotations are distinguished: in annotations, out annotations, and object constraints. The kind of an object annotation is determined syntactically by the way it refers to the program variables occurring in it (i.e. its constituent program variables; see 1.2): program variables and expressions may be modified by **in** or **out**, or may be unmodified. (See 4.13 for modifiers and modified expressions.)

- An object annotation is an *in annotation* if all its constituent program variables are modified by **in**. An in annotation contains neither the modifier **out** nor unmodified program variables. This kind of object annotation includes the case of an annotation that does not contain any program variable.

- An object annotation is an *out annotation* if it starts with the modifier **out**.

- An object annotation is an *object constraint* if it is not an out annotation and at least one constituent program variable is not modified by **in**.

An object annotation is elaborated by evaluating all expressions modified by **in** and substituting the resulting values in the boolean expression, as described in 4.13. Elaboration of an object annotation is thus equivalent to replacing each expression that is modified by **in** by a virtual constant which has been declared immediately before the object annotation and initialized to the value of that expression or variable. If the evaluation of an expression modified by **in** does not yield a defined value, the value of the annotation is undefined (see 4.14), and the Anna program in which it appears is inconsistent (see 1.3.3).

The meaning of an object annotation (i.e., its meaning after elaboration) is that it constrains the values of all its constituent program variables in certain computation states within its scope. The kind of the object annotation determines to which states the constraint applies.

An in annotation applies to the state upon entry to its scope, i.e. it constrains the *initial* value of its constituent program variables. Since elaboration is equivalent to replacing all program variables by their initial values, the (boolean) value of an elaborated in annotation expresses whether the constraint is satisfied or not.

An out annotation applies to the *final* computation state of its scope (see 1.3.1), i.e. it must be true upon normal exit from its scope. An out annotation is transformed to the Anna Kernel by placing it as an assertion (see 5.1) (a) at the end of the sequence of statements in its scope, (b) at the end of the sequence of statements of any exception handler in its scope, and (c) before every return, goto or exit statement that transfers control out of the scope of the out annotation.

An object constraint constrains every observable computation state within its scope. However, it constrains in a non-trivial way only after all constituent unmodified scalar program variables have been initialized: an object constraint has the default value TRUE in any state in which the value of an unmodified scalar program variable is not defined. This semantics is expressed in the transformation of an object constraint to the Anna Kernel by adding definedness premises. Details of this transformation are given in the following subsection.

*Examples of object annotations:*

```
      LIMIT : INTEGER := 10_000;
--|  - 2 ** in N ≤ LIMIT ≤ 2 ** (in N + 1);
--      Any value of LIMIT must satisfy the inequality bounds for the value of N
--      when the constraint is elaborated.
```

```
--:  function PRIME_BOUND(X : INTEGER) return INTEGER;
--|       where return Y : INTEGER => PRIME(Y) and 2 ** X < Y and
--|                     (for all Z : INTEGER => PRIME(Z) and 2 ** X < Z → Y ≤ Z);
      X : INTEGER := E;          --| X < PRIME_BOUND(E);
--      Values of X must be less than the smallest prime greater than 2**E.
```

*Example of an object annotation on two variables:*

```
      M, N : INTEGER := 0;       --| N ≤ M;
```

```
--      The values of N and M are constrained so that N is less than or equal to M in any
--      observable state throughout the scope of the annotation.
```

*Notes:*

The following properties of object annotations, which constitute differences between the Ada concept of constraint and Anna object constraints, should be noted:

- An object constraint in Anna constrains all its unmodified program variables. For example, an object constraint P(X, Y) constrains the aggregate of the pair of values of X and Y in each state to which the constraint applies.

- An object annotation may appear in any declarative part within the scopes of its constituent program variables. In particular, an object may be constrained in only part of its scope, and annotations on the same object can appear in more than one place. If more than one constraint is placed on an object, they need not be compatible in the Ada sense, that is, a new constraint need not imply a previous one (see also 3.3).

The smallest observable state transition in the scope of an object annotation is the execution of a simple statement (see 1.3.1). Thus an object constraint need not necessarily hold while a simple statement is being executed, for example during a procedure call. Note, however, that the set of observable states in the scope of an object annotation includes each state upon normal completion of the elaboration of each declaration in that scope (see 1.3.1).

If a modified program variable in an object annotation does not have a defined value in a state to which the annotation applies, the Anna program is inconsistent (see 1.3).

Since an out annotation constrains only the final state reached upon normal completion of the execution of its scope, such an annotation has no effect on consistency if the computation never completes normally, i.e. if the computation is non-terminating or propagates an exception (see 1.3.1). Note that "normal termination" includes normal termination of an exception handler in the scope.

3.2.1 Transformation of Object Constraints

An object constraint is transformed to the Anna Kernel by (a) adding definedness premises for unmodified constituent scalar variables and (b) distributing it over its scope.

The definedness premises make use of the attribute, DEFINED, provided in Anna for any object (see 3.5). An object constraint C, where X1, ..., Xn are the unmodified constituent scalar program variables, is first elaborated (as described above) and expanded to the conditional expression (see 4.12),

    **if** X1'DEFINED **and** ... **and** Xn'DEFINED **then** C **else** TRUE **end if;**

The original object constraint is then replaced by placing this expression as an assertion (see 1.3.2, 5.1) in the scope of C after every simple statement whose execution may have changed the value of one or more of the constituent program variables X1, ..., Xn. Similar assertions, with C replaced by **in** C, are placed at the point of the original object constraint and after any declaration in the scope of C whose elaboration may initialize or change the value of one or more of the constituent program variables, X1, ..., Xn.

This transformation of C into assertions is also applied to all bodies of subprograms and packages declared in the scope of C which may change the value of a constituent variables (as a global).

If a constituent scalar variable is an indexed component, e.g. has the form C(E), then the condition for the test whether all scalar variables have defined values is constructed so that C(E)'DEFINED is evaluated only if all variables occurring in E are defined. For example, an annotation

    A(K) > J;

where K and J are scalar variables, is transformed into a set of assertions using the expression,

    **if** (K'DEFINED **and then** A(K)'DEFINED) **and** J'DEFINED
        **then** A(K) > J **else** TRUE **end if;**

The conditional expression assertions that replace the original constraint are trivially true in the scope until all unmodified scalar program variables have been initialized. If the object constraint does not contain scalar program variables, no definedness premises are added, and the original constraint is distributed throughout its scope as described above.

In the transformation of object constraints to Anna Kernel assertions, a variable of a private type is treated according to the full type definition, i.e. a definedness premise is added if the private type is implemented as a scalar type (see 7.3.1).

*Example of a transformation of an annotation into a set of assertions:*

```
    declare
        A : array (1 .. 10) of INTEGER;
        J : NATURAL range 1 .. 10 := 1;
--|     A(J) = 1;
    begin
        loop
            A(J) := 1;
```

```
            exit when J = 10;
            J := J + 1;
        end loop;
    end;
```

The object constraint above is transformed into three assertions of the form,

if J'DEFINED and then A(J)'DEFINED then A(J) = 1 else TRUE end if;

placed at the location of the original object constraint and after the assignments to J and A(J) in the loop.

The first assertion holds since A(J)'DEFINED is false initially. After the assignment to A(J), both J'DEFINED and A(J)'DEFINED are true, and in addition A(J)=1 holds. After incrementing J, A(J)'DEFINED is again false. Therefore, the object constraint is satisfied everywhere in its scope.

*Notes:*

Definedness premises are not added for objects of composite types since their values need not be completely defined (see [Ada83, 7.6]). The attribute DEFINED may, however, be used explicitly to annotate composite objects (see 3.3).

The full details of transforming object annotations into assertions include a more complex case analysis than described here. For example, if in the scope of an object constraint one of its unmodified constituent variables is hidden by a local declaration, it is necessary to refer to the proper variable by other means, e.g by using an expanded name or by saving the value of the hidden variable locally in a virtual constant, and changing the assertions accordingly to refer to this expanded name or constant in place of the hidden variable. The exact details of the transformation are given in [18].

## 3.3 ANNOTATIONS OF TYPE AND SUBTYPE DECLARATIONS

A subtype annotation may be used to constrain a type or subtype. Such an annotation must immediately follow the full type declaration or subtype declaration of the (sub)type to be constrained; it is bound to that declaration by the reserved word **where**.

```
full_type_declaration ::=
        ... ada_full_type_declaration ...
        [ subtype_annotation ]

subtype_declaration ::=
        ... ada_subtype_declaration ...
        [ subtype_annotation ]

subtype_annotation ::=
        where [in out] identifier : type_mark => boolean_compound_expression ;
```

A subtype annotation follows the declaration of the (sub)type it annotates immediately; it is not possible to have more than one subtype annotation for any (sub)type. The type mark refers to the identifier introduced in the (sub)type declaration; it cannot appear in the compound expression. The identifier preceding the type mark is a logical variable of the annotated type; its scope extends to the end of the subtype annotation. All type marks occurring in the compound expression must refer to completely declared (sub)types other than the type being constrained.

A subtype annotation that contains the reserved words in out preceding the identifier is called a *modified subtype annotation*; this form may be used only to annotate types or subtypes declared in a package specification (i.e., in the visible or private parts) and is described in section 7.2.1.

A subtype annotation is elaborated by evaluating all constituent program variables and substituting the resulting values in the compound expression. Thus program variables have the same meaning as if they were modified by in. An elaborated subtype annotation is therefore equivalent to a subtype annotation in which each constituent program variable has been replaced by a virtual constant; this constant is declared in the same declarative part immediately preceding the (sub)type declaration, with the variable name as the expression initializing its value.

The meaning of a subtype annotation is that it restricts the domain of values of the (sub)type. Thus in,

```
subtype S is T;   --| where X : S => C(X);
```

the values in S are restricted to the set of all values X of type T that satisfy the condition, $C(X)$; the condition is also called the *type constraint* (or *subtype constraint*) on S. In general, this set of values is a proper subset of the set of values associated with the (sub)type in Ada.

A subtype of an annotated type inherits any constraint on the parent (sub)type. If the subtype is also annotated, the cumulative constraint placed on the subtype is the conjunction of the constraint expressed in its annotation and any inherited constraint; the conjunction describes an intersection of subsets of values of the (Ada) parent type. Successive constraints need not be compatible in the sense of Ada [Ada83, 3.3.2], that is, a subsequent constraint need not imply all previous constraints. A union of subsets can be obtained by disjunction of constraints in a subtype annotation.

A subtype annotation on a (sub)type constrains the values of any object declared of that (sub)type. This applies not only to constants and program variables but also to parameters, generic parameters, and logical variables in quantified expressions (see 4.11) or result annotations (see 6.5). A subtype annotation also constrains type conversions and qualified expressions involving the annotated type.

The following transformation provides the basis for reducing subtype annotations to the Anna Kernel and for runtime checking. A subtype annotation is transformed to a set of object annotations within its scope as follows. For each object of that (sub)type, an object constraint that corresponds to the type constraint is added at the point of the object declaration; for a formal parameter of a subprogram, the constraint is added to the subprogram annotation. The constraint for an object is constructed from the boolean expression of the (sub)type annotation by replacing all occurrences of the logical variable of that (sub)type declared immediately following the reserved word where by that object. Similarly, in quantified expressions containing declarations of logical variables of the (sub)type, the modified boolean expression is added to the constituent boolean expression for each logical variable of the (sub)type, as a premise in a universally quantified expression and as a conjunct in an existentially quantified expression. The modified boolean expression is also added to the result annotation of a function whose result is declared to be of the (sub)type, to the tests for membership in the (sub)type (see 4.5.2), and to type conversions (see 4.6) and qualified expressions (see 4.7).

The meaning of a modified subtype annotation differs from that of an unmodified subtype annotation only in the effect on variables of the annotated type: variables of that type have to satisfy the type constraint only outside of the package in which the subtype is declared. For details see 7.2.1.

*Examples of subtype annotations:*

```
    subtype EVEN is INTEGER;
--|     where X : EVEN => X mod 2 = 0;
--      The constraint on the type EVEN picks out the even values from the set of integers.
--      Since this is not a range, the constraint cannot be expressed as an Ada constraint.

    type DATE is
        record
            DAY   : INTEGER range 1 .. 31;
            MONTH : MONTH_NAME;
            YEAR  : INTEGER range 1 .. 4000;
        end record;
--|     where X : DATE => X.MONTH = "FEBRUARY" → X.DAY ≤ 29;
--      This could be expressed in Ada as a variant record type.

    type TABLE is array (NATURAL range <>) of ITEM;
    type QUEUE is
        record
            STORE     : TABLE(0 .. SIZE - 1);
            COUNT     : NATURAL range 0 .. SIZE := 0;
            IN_INDEX  : NATURAL range 0 .. SIZE - 1 := 0;
            OUT_INDEX : NATURAL range 0 .. SIZE - 1 := 0;
        end record;
--|     where Q : QUEUE =>
--|     Q.IN_INDEX = (Q.OUT_INDEX + Q.COUNT) mod SIZE;
--      This constraint on the record type cannot be expressed in Ada.

    type MATRIX is array (1 .. N, 1 .. N) of REAL;
    subtype DIAGONAL_MATRIX is MATRIX;
--|     where M : DIAGONAL_MATRIX =>
--|         for all I : range M'RANGE(1);
--|                 J : range M'RANGE(2) =>
--|                     (I ≠ J → M(I, J) = 0.0) and (I = J → M(I, J) ≤ MAX);
--      X is a program variable and is evaluated as part of the elaboration of the subtype
--      annotation. Note the use of quantification over the ranges. Such a constraint
--      cannot be expressed in Ada.
```

*Examples of successive subtype annotations:*

```
    subtype NATURAL is INTEGER;
--|     where X : NATURAL => X ≥ 0;


    subtype EVEN_NATURAL is NATURAL;
--|     where X : EVEN_NATURAL => X mod 2 = 0;
--      The subtype EVEN_NATURAL inherits the constraint of the type NATURAL
```

```
      subtype NATURAL_EVEN is INTEGER;
--|        where X : NATURAL_EVEN => X ≥ 0 and X mod 2 = 0;
--         The constraint on NATURAL_EVEN is the conjunction of the successive constraints
--         on NATURAL and EVEN_NATURAL so that the subtypes EVEN_NATURAL and
--         NATURAL_EVEN are equivalent in Anna (i.e., define the same subset of integer values)
```

*Notes:*

Since a subtype annotation restricts the set of values of a (sub)type it also affects the semantics of the test of membership in that (sub)type (see 4.5.2).

The object constraint imposed on an object by an annotation of its (sub)type is subject to the same rules as an object constraint that is stated directly. In particular, it is vacuously true as long as any constituent scalar variable does not have a defined value.

There is an important difference between the Ada notion of type constraint and Anna type annotations: Ada requires the constraints in successive subtype declarations to be compatible [Ada83, 3.3.2]; this is checked during elaboration. In Anna, type constraints can be arbitrary boolean expressions, for which mechanical compatibility checking during elaboration may not be possible in practice. Anna does not require successive constraints to be compatible. However, an inconsistency will be detected by verification or runtime consistency checking if a value is computed that is constrained by two constraints and satisfies only one of them.

*Example of incompatible successive subtype annotations:*

```
      subtype EVEN is INTEGER;
--|        where X : EVEN => X mod 2 = 0;

      subtype ODD_EVEN is EVEN;
--|        where X : ODD_EVEN => X mod 2 = 1;
--         No value can satisfy the combined constraints on EVEN and ODD_EVEN; thus
--         the set of values of subtype ODD_EVEN is empty. To check for this inconsistency
--         at elaboration would require automated deduction techniques using facts such as,
--         X mod 2=0 if and only if not (X mod 2=1). As soon as computation of a
--         value of ODD_EVEN is attempted the inconsistency will be detected by Anna
--         runtime checking.
```

3.3.1 - 3.3.2                    No additions

3.3.3 Operations on All Types

For every object A of any type, the following attribute is defined:

A'DEFINED    expresses whether the value of A is fully defined, i.e. whether A has received a value, if it is an object of a scalar type; or whether all components of A are fully defined, if A is an object of a composite type. For the exact meaning of DEFINED see the 3.5 for scalar types, 3.6.2 for arrays, 3.7.4. for records, and 3.8.2 for access types.

For every type T, the following attribute is defined:

T'INITIAL    denotes the initial value given by default to objects of type T. The initial value is the
             default initial value or default expression as given in the (sub)type definition of T, or
             null for access types. If no default is given (or defined by Ada), the value of the
             attribute is undefined.

*Notes:*

The attribute DEFINED is related to the Anna notion of definedness, but it expresses Anna
definedness only for scalar objects; see 4.14 for an explanation of the differences.

The main expected use of the attribute INITIAL is with private types, for which any default initial
value or default expression is not visible outside the package (see 7.4.2). For all other types, the
attribute may be considered a mere renaming of the default.


## 3.4 ANNOTATIONS OF DERIVED TYPES

A derived type inherits any constraint placed on its parent (sub)type. The declaration of a derived
type may be annotated further, like any other type declaration.

For an access type, the collection associated with the derived type is the same as that of the parent
type (see 3.8).


## 3.5 OPERATIONS OF SCALAR TYPES

For every scalar object X, the following boolean-valued attribute is defined:

X'DEFINED    expresses whether the variable X has a defined value. It is false if X has no initial value
             and becomes true when X receives a value by initialization, by an assignment, or by a
             call to a subprogram.

The attribute DEFINED is available for every scalar variable, including indexed components of arrays
and selected components of records. Thus, A(J)'DEFINED is true once the scalar array component
A(J) has received a value; similarly, for a selected component R.C of scalar type, the value of
R.C'DEFINED indicates whether the component has a defined value. (For the definition of the
attribute DEFINED of whole arrays or records see 3.6.2 and 3.7.4.)

For a formal parameter X of a scalar type, assumptions about the value of X'DEFINED in the
subprogram body can be derived from Ada semantics; for details see 6.2.

*Example:*

```
declare
     X : INTEGER;
```

```
        begin
--|         not X'DEFINED;
            X := 1;
--|         X'DEFINED;
            ...
        end;
```

*Note:*

The DEFINED attribute is also available for variables of a private type outside the package in which that type is declared, i.e., it is a visible operation of the private type. In this case, DEFINED has the meaning of the DEFINED attribute for the full definition of the private type (see 7.4).

## 3.6 ANNOTATIONS OF ARRAY TYPES

New names are introduced to denote states of array objects in annotations. The notation is based on sequences of assignment operations on arrays. Array states denote values of arrays. The state notation is similar to the named component notation for Ada aggregates except that a state associates a value with an object and represents a sequence of operations on the object resulting in its value.

### 3.6.1            No additions

### 3.6.2 Operations of Array Types

For every object A of an array type, the following attribute is defined:

A'DEFINED   is TRUE for an array A if for every component A(J,...,K) the attribute
            A(J,...,K)'DEFINED is TRUE. The attribute DEFINED is also defined for array slices.

*Example:*

```
        declare
            A : array (1 .. 10) of INTEGER;
        begin
            A(1) := - 1;
            A(2) :=   0;
--|         A(1)'DEFINED and A(2)'DEFINED and A(1 .. 2)'DEFINED;
--|         not A'DEFINED;
--          The annotations give the values of the DEFINED attribute after the second assignment.
        end;
```

*Note:*

A'DEFINED is TRUE if and only if X'DEFINED is TRUE for all subcomponents X of A. This differs from the *definedness* concept given in 4.14.

3.6.3              No additions


3.6.4 Array States

For every array type T, array states are defined as new names of type T:

```
array_state ::=
    array_name [array_store_operation {; array_store_operation}]

array_store_operation ::=
    expression {, expression} => expression
```

For an array type T, the state, $A[J_1, \ldots, J_n => C]$ where A is an object or state of type T, $J_1$ to $J_n$ are index values for the n dimensions of T, and C is a value of the component type of T, denotes the value of A resulting from its current value after the value of the component $A(J_1, \ldots, J_n)$ is replaced by C. States beginning with an array name, A, and containing sequences of more than one array store operation denote values of A after the corresponding sequence of changes to the values of its components. If the sequence of array store operations contains more than one replacement for the same component, the rightmost operation denotes the value of that component in the state.

An array aggregate value is denoted by an array state having a sequence of array store operations corresponding to the named component form of the aggregate. Note that the notation using the reserved word **others** is not permitted in array states.

Array states may be used in Anna as names, in particular in indexed components and slices. An indexed component, A(K), where A is an array state, denotes the value of the Kth component of A. A slice, A(L .. R), where A is an array state of a one-dimensional array, denotes a value.

*Examples of array states:*

```
    MY_SCHEDULE[TUESDAY => TRUE]
--      Denotes a value of MY_SCHEDULE after the TUESDAY component is set to TRUE.

    SPACE[INDEX_1 => E; INDEX_2 => F]
--      Denotes a value of the array SPACE after two array store operations.
```

*Examples of array states in annotations:*

```
    A, B : SCHEDULE := SCHEDULE'(others => FALSE);
    ...
    A(MONDAY)  := TRUE;
    B(TUESDAY) := TRUE;
--| A[TUESDAY => TRUE] = B[MONDAY => TRUE];
--      In the annotation, the array states denote values of A and B that would result from their
--      current values if the array store operations were performed.

    begin
        Y         := A(X);
        A(X)      := A(X + 1);
        A(X + 1)  := Y;
    end;
```

```
--|  A = in A[X => in A(X + 1); X + 1 => in A(X)];
--        The final value of A is denoted by a state resulting from two operations on the initial
--        value of A. The state represents the operations but not how they are achieved.
```

*Examples of an array state in an indexed component:*

```
MY_TABLE[3 => 16](3)                          --  Denotes the value 16;
MY_TABLE[3 => 16; 4 => 17; 3 => 18](3) --  = 18;
```

*Example of an annotation of a SWAP procedure specification using array states:*

```
     procedure SWAP(A : in out VECTOR; I, J : INDEX);
--|      where out (A = in A[I => in A(J); J => in A(I)]);
```

*Notes:*

Two array states are equal if they denote the same array value; the same value may be denoted by many different state expressions.

Array states satisfy the standard axiomatic relationship with array selection, e.g. in the one dimensional case:

$$I = J \rightarrow A[I => E](J) = E,$$
$$I \neq J \rightarrow A[I => E](J) = A(J)$$

This axiom expresses that the rightmost store operation gives the current value of a component.

The semantics of array states implies that $A[O;P] = A[O][P]$ where O, P are sequences of array store operations.

Array states denote values. They are not variable names and consequently may not appear on the left side of an assignment, nor as an **out** parameter of a procedure call.

## 3.7 ANNOTATIONS OF RECORD TYPES

New names are introduced for states of record objects in annotations. Record states denote values of records. The notation for record states is based on sequences of assignment operations on records. It is similar to the named component notation for Ada aggregates except that a state associates a value with an object and represents a sequence of operations resulting in the value.

### 3.7.1 - 3.7.3                    No additions

### 3.7.4 Operations of Record Types

For every variable R of a record type, the following boolean-valued attribute is defined:

R'DEFINED   is TRUE if for all components R.N, R.N'DEFINED is TRUE.

*Examples:*

```
    BIRTHDATE : DATE := DATE'(20, MAY, 1951);
--| BIRTHDATE'DEFINED = TRUE;

    declare
        type CELL;
        type LINK is access CELL;
        type CELL is
            record
                VALUE : INTEGER;
                SUCC  : LINK;
                PRED  : LINK;
            end record;

        HEAD : LINK;

    begin
                             --| HEAD.all'DEFINED = FALSE;
        HEAD.VALUE := 0; --| HEAD.all'DEFINED = TRUE;
        ...                  --   DEFINED is always TRUE for access type objects (see 3.8.2),
    end;                     --   so that all components of HEAD are now DEFINED.
```

*Note:*

For a record R, R'DEFINED differs from the *definedness* concept given in 4.14.


3.7.5 Record States

For every record type T, record states are defined as new names.

```
    record_state   ::=
        record_name[record_store_operation {; record_store_operation}]

    record_store_operation ::=
        component_simple_name => expression
```

Record states may be used as names, in particular in selected components.

For any record type, T, the state, R[N => C] where R is an object or state of type T, N is the name of a component of R, and C is a value of the corresponding component type, denotes the value of R resulting from its current value after the value of the component R.N is replaced by C.   The component R.N must exist for the corresponding variant.   States beginning with a record name, R, and containing sequences of more than one record store operation denote values of R after the corresponding sequence of changes have been made to its components.   If the sequence of record store operations contains more than one replacement for the same component, the rightmost operation denotes the value of that component in the state.

A record aggregate value is denoted by a record state having a sequence of record store operations corresponding to the named component form of the aggregate. Note that the **others** notation is not permitted in record states.

A selected component, R . N, where R is a record state, denotes the current value of the component N of R.

*Examples of record states:*

```
    BIRTHDATE[YEAR => BIRTHDATE.YEAR + 1]
--  A state denoting the value of BIRTHDATE after incrementing the YEAR component.

    type DEVICE is (PRINTER, DISK, DRUM);
    type STATE  is (OPEN, CLOSED);

    type PERIPHERAL(UNIT : DEVICE := DISK) is
        record
            STATUS : STATE;
            case UNIT is
                when PRINTER =>
                    LINE_COUNT : INTEGER range 1 .. PAGE_SIZE;
                when others =>
                    CYLINDER    : CYLINDER_INDEX;
                    TRACK       : TRACK_NUMBER;
            end case;
        end record;

    WRITER      : PERIPHERAL(PRINTER);
    MY_DISK     : PERIPHERAL;              --   Default discriminant is DISK.

    WRITER[LINE_COUNT => 1]
--  Denotes a value of the WRITER record with LINE_COUNT set to 1.

    MY_DISK[STATUS => OPEN; TRACK => 500; STATUS => CLOSED]
--  Denotes a value of a DISK record resulting from three operations.

    MY_DISK[LINE_COUNT => 50]
--  Illegal state since a LINE_COUNT component does not exist in PERIPHERAL(DISK).

    MY_DISK[TRACK => 500; UNIT => PRINTER; STATUS => OPEN; LINE_COUNT => 50]
--  Legal state denoting a value of a PRINTER record including a discriminant change.
```

*Examples of a record state in a selected component:*

```
    WRITER[LINE_COUNT => 1].LINE_COUNT = 1

    MY_DISK[STATUS => OPEN; TRACK => 500; STATUS => CLOSED].STATUS = CLOSED
```

*Notes:*

Record states satisfy the standard axiomatic relationship with record selection, e.g.

```
    R[N => E].N = E,
    R[N => E].M = R.M        if N and M are different component names.
```

Ada rules restricting changes to record discriminants imply that a store operation to a discriminant component occurs in a state only within a subsequence of store operations that corresponds to a complete aggregate value.

The semantics of record states implies that $R[O;P] = R[O][P]$ where O, P are sequences of record store operations.

## 3.8 ANNOTATIONS OF ACCESS TYPES

The objects designated by the values of an access type form a collection associated with that type. Operations performed on objects of an access type by an Ada program result in changes in the state of the associated collection. In many cases the results and effects (including side effects) of such programs are describable only by annotations on the state of the collection. Therefore Anna explicitly associates a collection state with each access type and introduces notation for collection states.

In Anna, an access type T has an attribute, T'COLLECTION, whose value at any point in a program is the current state of the collection that encapsulates the objects designated by values of T. The states of T'COLLECTION (i.e., its set of possible values) have the type, T'COLLECTION'TYPE. New names are introduced to denote states of the collection resulting from sequences of operations on the access objects of type T.

3.8.1                    No additions

3.8.2 Operations of Access Types

For every access type object, X, the following boolean-valued attribute is defined:

X'DEFINED    has the value TRUE. (*Note:* Since access type objects are always initialized to **null**, the DEFINED attribute always has the value TRUE; its definition is included for access types in order to complete the definition of this attribute for objects of all types.)

For every access type T, defined as,

   **type** T **is access** S;

the following attributes are defined:

T'COLLECTION             Denotes the current state of the *collection* of objects of type S designated by values of type T.

T'COLLECTION'TYPE        The type of the states of T'COLLECTION. This is treated as a private type except that the equality operator may be redefined. Objects of this type may be declared in virtual Ada text and used in annotations.

T'COLLECTION'INITIAL The initial state of T'COLLECTION after elaboration of the declaration of T, i.e., an empty collection.

C'NEXT                         For a prefix C that denotes a collection state of type T'COLLECTION'TYPE:
                               Yields the next value of type T to be allocated when the collection has state C.

If T1 is a subtype of access type T then the collection associated with T1 is the collection of T and may be referred to as T1'COLLECTION or as T1'BASE'COLLECTION.

T'COLLECTION is a dynamic attribute in the sense that its value changes during a computation. (*Note:* In Ada the COUNT, CALLABLE and TERMINATED attributes are dynamic.) In annotations it is treated as a program variable; its current value is used in elaboration of a type annotation and its occurrences in annotations may be modified by **in** and **out**. If it occurs unmodified in an object constraint, all of its states must satisfy the constraint within that scope. However, it must be noted that in (virtual) Ada text T'COLLECTION is an attribute, e.g. it may only occur in expressions or as an **in** parameter of a subprogram.

Operations in virtual text are not permitted if they change the state of the collection associated with an actual access type; for instance, expressions in annotations or virtual text may not contain an allocation of objects of an actual access type (see 1.1).

*Note:*

Anna provides a test for membership in collections (see 4.5.2, 3.8.4).


3.8.3 Constraints on Access Types

A subtype annotation may constrain an access type or subtype declaration just as for any other class of types (see 3.3). In the case of access (sub)type declarations most annotations will constrain the designated values and not the access values themselves. When an annotation on a subtype of an access type constrains only the designated values, any value of the original access type can be used to designate a value in the appropriate subset of values of the designated type. Therefore, in these cases, the set of access values of the subtype will be the same as the base type; runtime checks ensure that each access subtype value designates a constrained value. However, in Anna it is possible to constrain the set of values of an access subtype to be a subset of the base type by annotations using collections (see third example below).

*Examples of annotations on access types.*

        **type** FRAME **is access** MATRIX;

        **subtype** DIAGONAL_FRAME **is** FRAME;
--|        **where** X : DIAGONAL_FRAME => X.**all isin** DIAGONAL_MATRIX;
--         *The sets of access values of DIAGONAL_FRAME and FRAME are the same;*
--         *the values of DIAGONAL_FRAME are constrained to designate values of*
--         *DIAGONAL_MATRIX (see 3.3).*

```
     type T is access S;
-- |      where X : T => X = null;
--        T consists of the null value.

     subtype T1 is T;
-- |      where X : T1 => X isin T'COLLECTION;
--        Values in T1 are constrained to be those values of T that have been allocated at this point.
--        The set of values of T1 will usually be a subset of T; the state, T'COLLECTION, is evaluated
--        when the subtype declaration is elaborated, analogously to an Ada range constraint with
--        dynamic bounds. For the test of membership in a collection see 3.8.4.
```

*Note:*

Quantification over access types and collections is described in 4.11.

3.8.4 Collection States

For every access type T, collection states of type T'COLLECTION'TYPE are defined as new names:

```
collection_state ::=
    collection_name[collection_operation {; collection_operation}]

collection_operation ::=
      allocator
    | selected_component => expression
    | indexed_component  => expression
```

Collection states may be used in membership tests (see 4.5.2) and as names in indexed components. The meaning of collection states, tests of membership in collection states, and indexed components of collection states is described as follows.

Let X be an access object of type T, S be the type of objects designated by values of T, and let C be a collection state of type T'COLLECTION'TYPE.

C[ new S'(E)]     The collection state resulting from C by the evaluation of an allocator, **new** S'(E). Similarly for other forms of qualified expressions in allocators.

C[X.all => E]     The collection state resulting from C by a change to the object designated by X when an assignment, X.all := E, is executed. Similarly for selected components, C[X.F => E], and indexed components, C[X(J) => E], whenever the type S of designated objects permits these operations to be performed on X.

X isin C          Yields the value TRUE if X designates an object in C, otherwise returns FALSE. The test, X **not** isin C yields the complementary result (see 4.5.2). When C is the *current* collection state, i.e., C is T'COLLECTION, then X isin C is equivalent to X ≠ **null**.

C(X)              Denotes the value of the object designated by the value of X if X isin C is TRUE, and is undefined otherwise. For any access value X of type T, X.all is equivalent to T'COLLECTION(X), i.e., the index operation applied to the current collection state. Similarly for a selected or indexed component; e.g. X.F, denotes the same value as T'COLLECTION(X).F.

States containing sequences of more than one collection operation denote the state of the collection after the corresponding sequence of Ada operations has been performed on the objects of type T. If the sequence of collection operations contains more than one change of the complete object designated by an access value, the rightmost operation defines the value of the object designated by that access value in that state; similarly for multiple changes of a component of a designated object.

*Examples of collection states:*

```
T'COLLECTION[new S]
```
--          *The collection state resulting from the current state after an allocation,* **new** *S.*

```
T'COLLECTION[X.all => A]
```
--          *The collection state after* X.all := A.

```
T'COLLECTION[new S; X.all => A] and X = T'COLLECTION'NEXT
```
--          *The collection state and value of X after, X :=* **new** *S'(A); for expression A,*
--          *or after, X :=* **new** *S'A; for aggregate A. This can also be written as:*
--          *T'COLLECTION[new S'A] and X = T'COLLECTION'NEXT.*

```
LINK'COLLECTION[new CELL; HEAD.all => CELL'(0, null,null)]
and HEAD = LINK'COLLECTION'NEXT
```
--          *State of the collection associated with LINK that results from the*
--          *current state after allocation and initialization of HEAD, [Ada83, 3.8.1.]*

```
C[X.F => E]
C[X.all => X.all [F => E]]
```
--          *Alternative notations for the collection state that results by starting in state C*
--          *and performing the assignment, X.F := E;*

*Examples of membership tests and indexing on collection states:*

```
HEAD isin LINK'COLLECTION
```
--          *TRUE after declaration and initialization of HEAD, see [Ada83, 3.8.1].*
```
MY_CAR not isin CAR_NAME'COLLECTION
```
--          *TRUE after declaration and* **null** *initialization, [Ada83, 3.8.1].*

```
T'COLLECTION'NEXT isin T'COLLECTION[...; new S; ...]
```
--          *TRUE always*

```
LINK'COLLECTION[HEAD.all => CELL'(0, null,null)](HEAD).VALUE
```
--          *= 0.*

```
if X = C'NEXT then C[new T'E](X) = E endif
```
--          *is always TRUE.*

*Example of annotations on access variables*

```
type T is access S;
     X : T := new S'(A);
     Y : T := new S'(B);
```

```
--|              X ≠ Y and T'COLLECTION(X) = A;
```

*Example of annotation of a side effect:*

```
        declare
            U, V : T;
--|         out (T'COLLECTION =
--|             in T'COLLECTION[new S; U.all => A; U.all => B] and
--|             U = in T'COLLECTION'NEXT and
--|             T'COLLECTION(V) = B);
        begin
            U := new S'(A);
--|         U isin T'COLLECTION and V notisin T'COLLECTION;
            V := U;
            U.all := B;
        end;
--      In the final collection, U and V both designate the same object and its value is B.
```

*Examples of subprogram annotations on access type parameters:*

```
    type WORD;
    type LIST is access WORD;
    type WORD is record
                    ITEM : INTEGER;
                    NEXT : LIST;
                end record;
--      Values of type LIST designate linear lists of WORDs.

    procedure RESTRICTED_INSERTION(P : LIST; N : INTEGER);
--|         where out (LIST'COLLECTION = in LIST'COLLECTION[P.ITEM => N]);
--      See Comment 1.

    procedure SHIFT_LEFT_INSERT(P : LIST; N : INTEGER);
--|         where out (for all X : LIST =>
--|         if X isin (in LIST'COLLECTION) and
--|             REACHABLE(P, X, in LIST'COLLECTION)
--|         then
--|             X.NEXT = in LIST'COLLECTION(X).NEXT and
--|             if in LIST'COLLECTION(X).NEXT ≠ null
--|             then X.ITEM = in LIST'COLLECTION(X.NEXT).ITEM
--|             else X.ITEM = N end if
--|         else
--|             X.all = in X.all
--|         end if);
```

```
--      In the list of WORDs reachable from P, an ITEM in a designated WORD is replaced by the
--      ITEM in the next WORD if there is one, and by N otherwise;designated WORDs that are
--      not reachable from P are unchanged. See Comment 2.
```

*Comment 1.* This annotation must be true on completion of a call to RESTRICTED_INSERTION. It describes the desired effect of the procedure: the collection may be changed only in the ITEM component of the object designated by P.

*Comment 2.* This annotation must be true on completion of a call to SHIFT_LEFT_INSERT. The

**3.8 ANNOTATIONS OF ACCESS TYPES**

collection is used to express a *before* and *after* relationship over *all* designated objects — i.e., the quantification is over all *values* of type LIST (see 4.11). The annotation assumes (formulation of) a concept of reachability between values of type LIST (see Introduction).

For an object X of an access type T (either a program variable or a logical variable), the meaning of modifiers applied to indexed or selected components is given by applying the modifier to the equivalent operation on T'COLLECTION. Thus, in this example, **in** X.ITEM means **in** (LIST'COLLECTION(X).ITEM), which is equivalent to **in** LIST'COLLECTION (**in** X).ITEM if X is a program variable, and to **in** LIST'COLLECTION(X).ITEM if X is a logical variable (see 4.13).

*Notes:*

The collection of a subtype or a derived type is the same as that of its base type or parent type.

Notation for collection states satisfies C[O;P] $\triangleq$ C[O][P] where O and P are sequences of collection operations. Also, the use of selected and indexed components in collection operations provides alternative notations for the same state. For example, the two expressions,
```
    CAR_NAME'COLLECTION[MY_CAR.NUMBER => 123],
    CAR_NAME'COLLECTION[MY_CAR.all => MY_CAR.all[NUMBER => 123]]
```
denote the same state.

A collection has the same semantics as a data structure encapsulated in a package. Details of implementation are hidden in the collection package body and are not visible to the Anna programmer. The access type T behaves as a type exported from T'COLLECTION with visible selection or indexing operations.

The use of the COLLECTION attribute in annotations permits expression of constraints that are not expressible using the access type objects alone. It is however clear from recent research that other high level concepts associated with access types are needed in order to easily specify programs that use access types. In this respect the present access type facilities provided by Anna should be regarded as only a necessary basic set and not a sufficient set for all programs. Other annotation concepts may be defined by virtual subprograms with collection type parameters.

## 3.9 DECLARATIVE PARTS

Basic annotations may appear in the positions of basic declarative items in a declarative part. They may not be placed in the position of a later declarative item.

For virtual units, no body or private part needs to be supplied, in relaxation of the Ada rules. Similarly, if a body stub is given for a virtual unit (which may be used to annotate the unit further), a separate subunit containing the corresponding proper body need not be supplied.

The Ada rules that restrict use of an entity before elaboration of its full declaration or body (see [Ada83, 3.9]) apply also to its use in formal comments. By "use" we mean, more precisely, "use in an evaluation". In Anna, use in evaluation includes elaboration and evaluation of annotations, in addition to the Ada uses. During elaboration of an annotation, every expression modified by **in** is evaluated (see 3.2, 4.13); any occurrence of an entity name in an expression modified by **in** thus constitutes a use in the Anna sense. More generally, any occurrence of an entity in an annotation is a use whenever the annotation is evaluated, that is, whenever the annotation must be satisfied. For instance, a declarative **in** annotation must be satisfied at the point where it appears; thus any entity occurring in it is used in an evaluation at that point.

# 4. NAMES AND EXPRESSIONS IN ANNOTATIONS

## 4.1 NAMES IN ANNOTATIONS

The set of names in Ada is extended in Anna by special attributes, by selected components denoting result values of procedure calls (see 6.8), by modified names (see 4.13), and by names for states of arrays (see 3.6.4), records (see 3.7.5), collections (see 3.8.4) and packages (see 7.7.3).

```
name ::=
    ... ada_name ...
    | initial_name
    | state

state ::=
    array_state
    | record_state
    | collection_state
    | package_state

selector ::=
    ... ada_selector ...
    | function_call
```

**4.1.1 - 4.1.3**                    No additions

### 4.1.4 Attributes

Additional attributes are defined in Anna; see Appendix A and the relevant sections.

**4.2 - 4.3**                    No additions

## 4.4 EXPRESSIONS IN ANNOTATIONS

Expressions in annotations are extended by the logical implication and equivalence operators (see 4.5.1), the Anna membership test, **isin** (see 4.5.2), quantified expressions (see 4.11), conditional expressions (see 4.12), and modified expressions (see 4.13).

```
compound_expression ::=
    expression [implication_operator expression]
    | quantified_expression
```

```
relation ::=
    ... Ada_relation ...
    | simple_expression [not] isin range
    | simple_expression [not] isin type_mark
    | simple_expression [not] isin collection_state

primary ::=
    ... ada_primary ...
    | conditional_expression
    | initial_expression
    | ( compound_expression )
```

*Note:*

The syntactic category compound_expression has been added in Anna to give implication operators a lower precedence than logical operators. Throughout this manual, the terms "expression" and "subexpression", when used without further qualification, refer to all kinds of Anna expressions, including compound expressions.


## 4.5 OPERATORS AND EXPRESSION EVALUATION

```
implication_operator ::=
    → | ↔
```

Evaluation of Anna expressions follows the rules for evaluation of Ada expressions. In particular, operators at the same level are associated in textual order from left to right, and operators are evaluated in some order that is not defined by the language.

The value of an expression formed by means of an operator is defined if and only if the value of each operand is defined (see 4.14).

Anna expressions are always evaluated in a particular state, which provides the values for the constituent program variables of the expression to be evaluated.

*Note:*

Evaluation of Anna expressions is a non-trivial extension of Ada expression evaluation. For most Anna expressions, the value can be established by computing it, following the Ada rules of evaluating expressions. However, for some extensions of Ada expressions, like quantified expression (see 4.11) and successor states (see 7.7.3), such computation rules are not readily available (and evaluation of such expressions may not be supported by Anna implementations). For the purpose of runtime consistency checking, this document defines transformations into executable Ada code; the value of an Anna expression may, however, also be established by means of formal reasoning. The language itself does not make any assumptions about how the value of an Anna expression is established.

### 4.5.1 Logical Operators

In addition to the Ada logical operators, Anna provides operators for logical implication and equivalence.

| Operator | Operation | Operand Type | Result Type |
|----------|-----------|--------------|-------------|
| $\rightarrow$ | implication | BOOLEAN | BOOLEAN |
| $\leftrightarrow$ | equivalence | BOOLEAN | BOOLEAN |

The implication operator $\rightarrow$ has the usual mathematical meaning.

A $\leftrightarrow$ B is defined as (A $\rightarrow$ B) **and** (B $\rightarrow$ A).

*Notes:*

$\rightarrow$ and $\leftrightarrow$ have the meaning of $\leq$ and = on boolean expressions; however, their precedence is the lowest of all operators allowed in boolean-valued expressions and subexpressions.

*Example of an equivalence operator:*

```
ST1 = ST2 ↔ ST1.INDEX = ST2.INDEX
     is equivalent to
(ST1 = ST2 → ST1.INDEX = ST2.INDEX) and
(ST1.INDEX = ST2.INDEX → ST1 = ST2)
```

### 4.5.2 Relational Operators and Membership Tests

Equality and inequality are predefined in annotations for all types including limited private types. The Anna predefined equality is the Ada predefined equality whenever the latter is defined, and in all other cases it is the identity relation on values. Equality of limited private types may be redefined explicitly, as in Ada; however, Anna imposes additional restrictions (see 7.4.4). Equality may also be redefined on package state types and collection state types even though they are not limited types (see 3.8.2, 7.7.1).

As a matter of convenience, a conjunction of relations may be written in Anna as a sequence of relations:

A *op1* B *op2* C     *is equivalent to*     (A *op1* B **and** B *op2* C)

*Example of a sequence of relational operators:*

```
S ≤ SQRT(N) < S + 1
     is equivalent to
S ≤ SQRT(N) and SQRT(N) < S + 1
```

Anna provides two kinds of membership tests that are predefined for all types: the Ada membership tests **in** and **not in,** and the Anna membership tests **isin** and **not isin.** The Ada membership tests may be used in virtual text, but not in annotations. The Anna membership tests are for use in annotations and virtual text.

The Ada membership test has its standard Ada meaning in Anna:  X in T is true in Anna if the value of X belongs to the set of values denoted by the type mark T in Ada. However, the set of values of a type or subtype may be restricted in Anna by a subtype annotation (see 3.3); the Ada membership test is evaluated without reference to annotations. Therefore, the test X in T may have the value TRUE in cases where the annotation of T imposes an additional constraint that is not satisfied. In this case the Ada test is inconsistent with the type annotation.

The checking method transforms Ada membership tests by adding virtual code to detect inconsistent tests and raise the exception ANNA_ERROR. For example, within the scope of an annotated subtype declaration of the form,

```
subtype T is S;  --| where X : T => C(X);
```

an if-statement,

```
if Y in T then A end if;
```

is transformed to,

```
if Y in T then
--: if not C(Y) then raise ANNA_ERROR; end if;
    A;
end if;
```

The Anna membership test X isin T has the value TRUE if X belongs to the set of values denoted by T and also satisfies any type annotation of T; otherwise the test has the value FALSE. The test not isin gives the complementary result to the membership test isin.

In addition to membership in a (sub)type, Anna provides a test for membership in a collection associated with an access type (see 3.8.4): If X is an object of a access type T, then X isin T has the value TRUE if the value of X designates an object in T'COLLECTION, and FALSE otherwise.

*Note:*

Equality on private types may be redefined explicitly in Anna (see 6.7 and 7.7.1).


4.5.3 - 4.5.7                     No additions


## 4.6 TYPE CONVERSIONS

If the type indicated by the type mark in a type conversion is subject to a type constraint, then the value of the expressions given as the operand of the type conversion must satisfy that constraint. If such a constraint is not satisfied, the program in which the type conversion occurs is inconsistent; in this case the runtime checking of consistency of the type conversion will raise the exception ANNA_ERROR.

## 4.7 QUALIFIED EXPRESSIONS

If the type indicated by the type mark in a qualified expression is subject to a type constraint, then the value of the operand must satisfy that constraint. If such a constraint is not satisfied, the program in which the qualified expression occurs is inconsistent; in this case runtime consistency checking of the qualified expression will raise the exception ANNA_ERROR.


## 4.8 - 4.10                    No additions


## 4.11 QUANTIFIED EXPRESSIONS

Quantified boolean expressions in Anna generalize the classical first order logic meaning of quantifiers.

```
quantified_expression ::=
    quantifier domain {; domain} => boolean_compound_expression

domain ::=
        identifier_list : subtype_indication
    |   identifier_list : range

quantifier ::=
    [not] for all | [not] exist
```

The identifiers in the domain of a quantifier are called *logical variables* and are said to be *declared* in the domain of the quantifier. When the quantifier domain is defined by a range, the type of the logical variables is the base type of the range. The scope of a logical variable extends from its occurrence in the domain to the end of the (boolean) compound expression following the symbol => . A logical variable is visible and can be used in the subsequent compound expression, but not in the subtype indications or range of the quantifier domain(s). For example, in an expression of the form

**for all** X : S => P(X) **and** (**exist** Y : T => Q(X,Y))

the logical variable X is visible in the subexpressions P(X) and Q(X,Y) and the subtype indication T, whereas Y is visible only in Q(X,Y). As in ordinary object declarations, a logical variable hides any previously declared object with the same name. Thus a quantifier domain of the form X : INTEGER **range** 1 .. X is illegal.

The classical interpretation of quantified boolean expressions requires that all subexpressions in the scope of a quantifier always have a value. Since expressions in Anna contain the set of Ada expressions it is clear that a subexpression may be undefined. In Anna, a quantification has a meaning even when the boolean expression in its scope is not defined for all values in its domain (definedness of expressions is explained in 4.14).

The logical variables are interpreted as ranging over the set of values of the indicated subtype. Quantified boolean expressions have the following meaning in Anna.

**for all** X : T => P(X) *means*     "for all values X of (sub)type T such that P(X) is defined, P(X) is true".

**exist** X : T => P(X) *means*     "there exists a value X of (sub)type T such that P(X) is defined and true".

If P(X) is defined for every value X in T, then (typed) quantification has the same meaning in Anna as in classical logic. The quantified expressions have defined values even if P(X) is undefined for some value in T. In fact, **for all** X : T => P(X) is true if and only if there exists no value X in T for which P(X) is both defined and false. Thus the generalized interpretation of quantification in Anna preserves the standard relationship between the quantifiers, i.e.,

**for all** X : T => P(X)     *is equivalent to*     **not exist** X : T => **not** P(X).

*Examples of quantified expressions:*

**for all** X : DAY => DAY'IMAGE(X)'LENGTH = 3;
`--`     *See [Ada83, 3.5.1].*

**for all** X : DAY => **exist** P : PERSON_RECORD => P.BIRTHDATE.DAY = X;
`--`     *This quantified expression is true since for any of the seven values of DAY*
`--`     *there is a record aggregate of the type PERSON_RECORD with a BIRTHDATE*
`--`     *component having that value as DAY component.*

**for all** N : NATURAL => **exist** S : NATURAL => S $\leq$ SQRT(N) < S + 1;

*Notes:*

Note that in the presence of undefined expressions the conjunction of quantified expressions,

(1)     (**for all** X : T => A(X)) **and** (**for all** X : T => B(X))

is *not* necessarily equivalent to the similar quantified expression,

(2)     **for all** X : T => A(X) **and** B(X).

For instance, in the case where for all values X in T either A(X) or B(X) is undefined, the expression (2) is true whereas the quantified conjunction (1) is false if A(Y) is defined and false for at least one value Y in T (see also 4.14).

Quantification in Anna is always over a finite (though potentially very large) set of values since Ada assumes the existence of (implementation-dependent) bounds for discrete types. This is the basis for the transformation of quantified expressions into checking code discussed in 4.11.1.

Quantification over a private type is interpreted as quantification over the set of values defined by the full declaration of the type.

Quantification over an access type is interpreted (as with any other class of type) as quantification over the set of values of that type, i.e., the set of all possible access values. In Anna quantification is defined only over sets of values of a type. However it is possible to construct expressions using quantification over an access type that are equivalent to quantification over the set of designated objects in the associated collection. For example,

>     for all X : T => P( X . all )

is interpreted in Anna (see 3.8.4) as

>     for all X : T => P( T'COLLECTION(X) );

since X isin T'COLLECTION is true if and only if T'COLLECTION(X) is defined, the quantified expression above will be true exactly if P(V) is true for the values V of all objects in the collection.

*Example:*

>     **type** PERSON_POINTER **is access** PERSON_RECORD;

`--`    *The following two quantified expressions are equivalent (see 3.8.4):*

>     **for all** X : DAY => **exist** P : PERSON_POINTER => P.BIRTHDATE.DAY = X;

>     **for all** X : DAY => **exist** P : PERSON_POINTER =>
>         PERSON_POINTER'COLLECTION(P).BIRTHDATE.DAY = X;

`--`    *The value of these expressions depends on the values of objects in the collection.*

### 4.11.1 Transformation of Quantified Expressions into the Anna Kernel

For the purpose of checking, an Anna quantified expression is translated into a call to a virtual Ada function that performs the check for all elements of a type indicated in the domain of the quantifier. The order in which the checking function steps through the values in the type is the usual increasing order for discrete types; the order is unspecified for non-discrete types.

- **for all** X : T => P(X) is transformed into a call to the function CHECK_P_FOR_ALL, defined as follows:

```
        function CHECK_P_FOR_ALL return BOOLEAN is
        begin
            for X in T loop --   in some arbitrary order if T is not discrete
                begin
                    if not P(X) then return FALSE; end if;
                exception
                    when others => null;
                end;
            end loop;
            return TRUE;
        end;
```

● **exist** X : T => P(X) is transformed into a call to the function CHECK_P_EXIST, defined
  as follows:

```
function CHECK_P_EXIST return BOOLEAN is
begin
    for X in T loop --    in some arbitrary order if T is not discrete
        begin
            if P(X) then return TRUE; end if;
        exception
            when others => null;
        end;
    end loop;
    return FALSE;
end;
```

*Note:*

Note that if the evaluation of P(X) raises an exception, which implies P(X) is undefined, the checking
continues. If computation of P(X) terminates (normally or exceptionally) for all values X, the result
returned by the checking function is equivalent to the value of the original quantified expression.

The definition of the above checking functions assumes that the standard Ada meaning of the loop
construct is extended for iteration over values of non-discrete types. It is implementation dependent
for which types evaluation of quantified expressions during consistency checking is actually
performed.


## 4.12 CONDITIONAL EXPRESSIONS

A conditional expression selects one of a number of expressions for evaluation, depending on the
truth value of one or more corresponding conditions in the same way an if statement in Ada selects a
sequence of statements for execution.

```
conditional_expression ::=
    if condition then
        compound_expression
    {elsif condition then
        compound_expression}
    else
        compound_expression
    end if

condition ::=
    boolean_compound_expression
```

All expressions must have the same base type. For the evaluation of a conditional expression, the
condition following **if** and any conditions following an **elsif** are evaluated in sequence until one
evaluates to TRUE or the **else** has been reached; then the corresponding expression is evaluated.

*Examples of conditional expressions:*

> **if** X ≠ 0 **then** Y / X * X = Y **else** Y * X = 0 **end if**
> -- *This conditional expression is defined, even though*
> -- *the subexpression after* **then** *is not always defined*

> A[I => E](J) = **if** I = J **then** E **else** A(J) **end if**
> -- *The conditional expression implies the two formulas:*
> -- I = J → A[I => E](J) = E
> -- I ≠ J → A[I => E](J) = A(J)

*Notes:*

In contrast to Ada if statements, conditional expressions must contain an **else** part. Otherwise evaluation of a conditional expression might "fall through" all conditions and not return any value.

Conditional expressions have been introduced into Anna to permit a programmer to construct defined annotations from partially defined expressions. The classical interpretation of the logical operators requires that both A and B have defined values in order for expressions such as A **or** B or A → B to have defined values; they can therefore not be used to define an operator with the semantics of conditional expressions. The Ada short-circuit control forms **and then** and **or else** are special forms of such an operator for boolean-valued expressions; expressions containing **and then** or **or else** may be regarded as special cases of conditional expressions:

> Q **and then** P     *is the same as*     **if** Q **then** P **else** FALSE **end if**
> Q **or else** P      *is the same as*     **if** Q **then** TRUE **else** P **end if**.

## 4.13 MODIFIERS

The execution of a program can be formally modeled as a sequence of state transitions (see 1.3.1). At each transition, the values of program variables may change. In general an annotation containing program variables refers to all computation states that may be observed during execution in its scope. The modifiers **in** and **out** refer to the *initial* and *final* states of a computation (see also 3.2).

```
initial_name ::=
    in simple_name

initial_expression ::=
    in (compound_expression)
```

The expression following a modifier **in** or **out** is said to be *modified by* that modifier; similarly, all constituent variables of a modified expression are considered to be modified by that modifier. The modifier **in** may be applied to a simple name or a parenthesized compound expression. The modifier **out** may be applied only to a primary term, and, as a consequence of the Anna syntax rules, can only appear at the beginning of an object annotation (see 3.2).

Initial expressions may appear inside an expression modified by **out**. Modifiers may not be applied to logical variables. More precisely, the simple name in an initial name may not be a logical variable, and an expression modified by **in** or **out** may not contain an occurrence of a logical variable, unless it includes the full scope of the logical variable, e.g. the whole quantified expression in which the logical variable is declared. (In the terminology of logic, a logical variable may not occur *free* in an initial expression.)

The modifiers **in** and **out** are used to modify the semantics of expressions depending on the scope of the annotation in which they appear: the modifier **in** refers to the *initial* state in the scope, the modifier **out** to the *final* state (see 1.3.1 for the definition of initial and final state in a scope). **in** V, where V is a simple variable name, denotes the initial value of V, i.e., the value of V in the initial state, and an initial expression, **in** ( E ) denotes the initial value of the (compound) expression E. Similarly, **out** E denotes the final value of a primary E. The modifier **out** can be used only in an out annotation, which applies to the final state of its scope (see 3.2).

The effect of the modifier **in** on the meaning of expressions in annotations is made precise by the rules for elaboration of annotations. Annotations are elaborated upon entry to their scope. During elaboration, every occurrence of **in** V in an annotation is replaced by the value of V on entry to the scope. Replacement of an initial value is equivalent to declaring a virtual constant of appropriate type,

```
--: IN_V : constant T := V;
```

at the beginning of the scope of the annotation, intializing it with the value of the variable, and then replacing all occurrences of **in** V in the annotation by in_V. Similarly, an expression **in** ( E ) is replaced by the initial value of E in the scope of the annotation, provided E does not contain logical variables. Thus, the elaboration of an annotation removes all occurrences of the modifier **in**. For example, elaboration of an out annotation of the form **out** ( X = **in** E ), where E is some expression, will result in an annotation of the form **out** ( X = C ) for some constant C.

If evaluation of an expression modified by **in** does not yield a defined value, the value of the annotation in which the expression occurs is undefined (see 4.14), and the Anna program in which it appears is inconsistent (see 1.3.3).

*Examples of modified expressions in object annotations:*

```
    X, Y : INTEGER;
    . . .
--| X ** 2 + Y ** 2 ≤ in X ** 2 + in Y ** 2;
--    Throughout the scope of the annotation, the sum of squares of X and Y is bounded
--    by the sum of squares of their initial values.

--| out (X ** 2 + Y ** 2 ≤ in (X ** 2 + Y ** 2));
--    The sum of squares of in values is an upper bound of the sums of squares of out values.
--    Note that this annotation is a consequence of the previous annotation.

    C : COLOR; --| C = in C0;
--    The annotation expresses constancy of the variable C,
--    in particular it implies out (C = in C0);
```

*Example of a type annotation with an implicit* **in** *modifier:*

```
    type FUNNY is array (1 .. MAX) of INTEGER;
--|      where A : FUNNY =>
--|          for all I : INTEGER range 1 .. MAX =>
--|              I mod 2 = 0 → A(I) ≤ MAX;
--       All occurrences of MAX in the annotation are elaborated in the same way as in the
--       type declaration. Thus MAX is treated as if it were modified by in (see 3.3).
```

*Example of modifiers in a procedure specification:*

```
    procedure SORT(A : in out INTEGER_VECTOR);
--|      where out (PERMUTATION(A, in A) and ORDERED(A));
--       This out annotation expresses that the out value of A must be a permutation
--       of its in value and that the out value of A is ordered.
```

*Notes:*

As a consequence of the syntax rules, the modifier **in** applies only to A in an expression of the form **in** A(J), which is in general not equivalent to **in** (A(J)). The expression **in** A(J) denotes the component of the initial value of the array A indexed by the (current) value of J, whereas **in**(A(J)) denotes the component of the initial value of A indexed by the initial value of J.

Elaboration of annotations may involve evaluation of arbitrarily complex initial expressions, just as elaboration of Ada declarations may involve arbitrarily complex computations. However, the value of an Anna expression cannot always be determined by straightforward computation (see 4.5); thus elaboration of annotations, like evaluation of Anna expressions in general, may in some cases depend on formal reasoning.

## 4.14 DEFINEDNESS OF EXPRESSIONS

The value of an Ada expression may not be defined, for example, if the expression contains an uninitialized variable, or its evaluation raises an exception or never terminates. Similarly, the value of an expression in an annotation may or may not be defined. An expression in Anna is considered *defined* if it is a legal Anna term and its evaluation terminates normally; otherwise it is called *undefined*. The following rules formalize this intuitive notion of definedness for Anna expressions.

1. A constant is defined (uninitialized constants are not legal in Ada); a deferred constant is defined after its full declaration.

2. A logical variable is defined.

3. A scalar program variable X is defined if it is initialized, i.e., if X'DEFINED has the value TRUE (see 3.5).

4. A non-scalar program variable is defined. A collection state is defined after elaboration of the access type; the current state of a package is defined after elaboration of the package body.

5. An indexed component is defined if all index expressions are defined and satisfy any Ada or Anna constraint on the index types, and the object it denotes is defined according to these rules.

6. A selection on a collection, C(X), is defined if X designates an object in C, i.e. X **isin** C is true, and the designated object is defined according to these rules.

7. A conditional expression is defined if all evaluated conditions are defined and the selected expression corresponding to the first condition that is true is also defined.

8. A quantified expression is defined.

9. All Ada and Anna operators are considered strict, i.e. an expression formed with an operator symbol is defined only if all operands are defined.

10. A membership test X **isin** T is defined if X is defined and either T is an Ada (sub)type without type annotation, or T is constrained by a predicate C and C(X) is defined.

11. A call to a function is defined if it satisfies the following requirements:

    • The actual parameter expressions are defined;

    • they satisfy the in annotations of the function;

    • execution of the function body terminates normally, and the returned value satisfies the result annotations of the function.

12. For a visible subprogram P of a package, a call to a function attribute of P (see 6.8), i.e. a package state of the form S.P'NEW_STATE(X) (a successor state, see 7.7.3) or a record of out values S.P'OUT(X), is defined if the actual parameters, X, and the package state S satisfy the following requirements:

    • They are defined.

    • They satisfy the in annotations of the subprogram P.

    • Execution of the subprogram body of P with the expressions, X, as parameters terminates normally, and the values of the out and in out parameters (including the package state) on exit from the subprogram body satisfy the out annotations.

*Examples:*

```
X/X                              --   is undefined for  X = 0.
for all X : INTEGER => X/X = 1   --   is defined and true even though the
                                 --   expression following => is
                                 --   undefined for  X = 0.
```

*Example of consistent Anna text with undefined expressions in annotations:*

```
--   An array A with index range 1 to N is initialized,
     J := 1;
     loop --| for all I : INTEGER range 1 .. J - 1 => A(I) = I;
--   the loop invariant
         A(J) := J;
         exit when J = N;
         J := J + 1;
     end loop;
```

*Note on example:*

After J cycles in the loop, $A(I)$ is defined for $I \leq J$ and undefined for $I > J$. The loop invariant may equivalently be expressed by

```
     for all I : INTEGER range 1 .. N => A(I) = I;
```

since $A(I)$ is undefined for $I > J$ and does not affect the value of the quantified expression; thus the two quantified expressions are equivalent. An invariant that explicitly expresses which elements of A are initialized in a given state can be expressed by using the attribute DEFINED:

```
     for all I : INTEGER range 1..J - 1 => A(I)'DEFINED and then A(I) = I.
```

*Example of definedness of a function call:*

```
     function BINARY_SEARCH(A   : in INTEGER_VECTOR;
                            KEY : in INTEGER) return INTEGER;
--|      where
--|          in (SORTED(A)),
--|          return I : INTEGER => A(I) = KEY,
--|          (for all I:INTEGER range A'RANGE=> A(I) ≠ KEY) => raise NOT_FOUND;
     ...
     X := BINARY_SEARCH(A,1);
--       Right side expression is defined if the call is legal, A is sorted (the in condition),
--       the execution of the call terminates normally, and the returned value is the
--       index of a component having the KEY value.
```

For an example on definedness of successor states see 7.7.3.

*Notes:*

Note the relationship between definedness and the attribute DEFINED: for a scalar object, X, the rules given above state that X is defined exactly when X'DEFINED is true, whereas a composite object Y is always considered defined regardless of the value of Y'DEFINED.

The concept of definedness is central to giving meaning to annotations in Anna. As explained in Section 1.3, consistency of an annotation with underlying Ada text requires the annotation to be defined and true in all states to which it applies; annotations with undefined values or with value FALSE are considered inconsistent. Note, however, that object constraints are satisfied by default as long as the value of any constituent scalar program variable is still undefined (see 3.2).

Definedness of a function call or a package state involving a subprogram call depends on whether execution of the subprogram call terminates normally, in addition to the input and output parameter values satisfying all constraints imposed by annotations. In the context of formal reasoning about Anna programs, however, one only considers the subprogram specification and its annotation and does not take into account actual execution of the subprogram body. A function call may be said to be defined if the input parameter values satisfy the subprogram annotation and there is a possible set of values for the output parameters that satisfies the output annotations. The axiomatic semantics of Anna are based on the latter definition.

# 5. STATEMENT ANNOTATIONS

Statement annotations are basic annotations appearing in a sequence of statements. This chapter describes statement annotations in general, and properties of loop statement annotations in particular. Annotations of subprogram calls are described in Chapter 6, and of raise statements in Chapter 11.

## 5.1 ANNOTATIONS OF SIMPLE AND COMPOUND STATEMENTS

```
simple_statement ::=
    ... ada_simple_statement ...
    | basic_annotation_list

compound_statement ::=
    [compound_statement_annotation]
    ... ada_compound_statement ...

compound_statement_annotation ::=
    with
        basic_annotation_list
```

A statement annotation is either a simple statement annotation or a compound statement annotation. A *simple statement annotation* is a list of basic annotations in a statement position; an object annotation in the basic annotation list of a simple statement annotation is also called an *assertion* (see also 1.3.2). A *compound statement annotation* is a list of basic annotations that follows the reserved word **with** and precedes a compound statement.

The scope of a statement annotation is a statement. The scope of a simple statement annotation is the immediately preceding statement. The scope of a compound statement annotation is the immediately following compound statement. A simple statement annotation at the beginning of a sequence of statements or following a label is considered to have a null statement at that position as its scope.

Elaboration of a statement annotation takes place immediately before execution of the statement in its scope. Elaboration involves evaluating all expressions modified by **in**, as described for object annotations in 3.2.

The meaning of an assertion is that it must be true after execution of the statement in its scope if control of the computation then passes its position (i.e., a statement in that position would be executed next). The meaning of an assertion is the same as if its expression was modified by **out**. The meaning of a result annotation in a simple statement annotation is defined in 5.8 and 6.5, that of a propagation annotation in 11.4.

A compound statement annotation expresses constraints that must hold during the execution of the statement in its scope. More precisely, the constraints must be satisfied by all observable states (see 1.3.1) in the scope. A compound statement annotation is equivalent to the same list of basic annotations in the declarative part of a block statement whose body is the given statement.

Transformation of compound statement annotations into the Anna Kernel uses this equivalence: a compound statement with an annotation that does not consist only of in and out annotations is transformed into a block having that statement as body and the basic annotation list from the compound statement annotation as the declarative part.

*Examples of statement annotations:*

```
    X := X + 1;  --| X = in X + 1;
--          This annotation is equivalent to out (X = in X + 1);

    if A(X) > A(X + 1) then
        Y          := A(X + 1);
        A(X + 1) := A(X);
        A(X)       := Y;
    end if;
--|       A(X) ≤ A(X + 1);
--        Note that A(X) ≤ A(X + 1) is not always true during execution of the statement, for
--        example, before or after the first assignment, so this annotation cannot be
--        made part of a compound statement annotation unless modified by out.

--| with
--|       in LOW ≤ LOW and HIGH ≤ in HIGH;
    while LOW < HIGH loop
        MID := (LOW + HIGH) / 2;
        if X > A(MID) then
            LOW := MID + 1;
        else
            HIGH := MID;
        end if;
    end loop;
--        The constraint on LOW and HIGH must be true throughout the execution
--        of the loop body.
```

*Note:*

An **out** annotation of a compound statement can be expressed either as part of a compound statement annotation or as an assertion following the statement. Note the semantic difference between the two forms of annotations: an **out** annotation in a compound statement annotation applies to all exits from the statement, including those resulting from executing a goto statement, whereas an assertion constrains only final states corresponding to the textual end of the compound statement.

Note the difference between a declarative object constraint and an assertion: an object constraint in a declarative part applies to all (observable) states in its scope, whereas an assertion applies only to the final state.

**5.2 - 5.4**                               No additions

## 5.5 ANNOTATIONS OF LOOP STATEMENTS

An assertion inside a loop acts as an inductive assertion in the sense of the Hoare *invariant* [7]: the assertion must hold each time the annotated statement is executed within the loop. A compound statement annotation that has a loop statement as its scope constrains the computation states of the loop after the execution of each simple statement in the loop body; these annotations are more correctly called "loop invariants".

*Examples of annotations on a binary search loop statement:*

```
--|  with
--|      in LOW ≤ LOW and HIGH ≤ in HIGH,
--|      LOW ≤ MID + 1 and MID ≤ HIGH,
--|      ORDERED(A, in LOW, in HIGH),
--|      (ISININTERVAL(X, A, in LOW, in HIGH)
--|                                   → ISININTERVAL(X, A, LOW, HIGH));
--       These object constraints must be true throughout the execution of the loop body.
     while LOW < HIGH loop
         MID := (LOW + HIGH) / 2;
         if X > A(MID) then
             LOW := MID + 1;
         else
             HIGH := MID;
         end if;
     end loop;
```

*Example of an annotation inside a loop in a Square Root program:*

```
     declare
         X   : INTEGER := A;      --| A > 0;
         U,V : INTEGER := 0;
         W   : INTEGER := 1;
     begin
         loop
             V := V + W;
--|          U ** 2 ≤ X and V = (U + 1) ** 2 and W = 2 * U + 1;
             exit when V > X;
             U := U + 1;
             W := W + 2;
         end loop;
--       Notice that the loop annotation is not true of every execution state of the loop. It is
--       true after each execution of the first loop statement; this may be proved by induction.
     end;
```

*Notes:*

Care should be taken to distinguish between those annotations that constrain particular states during execution of the loop and those that must remain invariant over all states observable during execution of the loop. In general clarity of documentation and ease of proof are both aided by placing an annotation in the largest possible scope.

58

**5.6 - 5.7**                     No additions


## 5.8 ANNOTATIONS OF RETURN STATEMENTS

A result annotation on a return statement constrains the value returned by that statement (see 6.5).


**5.9**                     No additions

# 6. ANNOTATION OF SUBPROGRAMS

This chapter describes annotations of subprogram declarations, bodies and subprogram calls. It also introduces some attributes of subprograms which are useful in annotations.

## 6.1 ANNOTATIONS OF SUBPROGRAM DECLARATIONS

Subprogram annotations are basic annotations that follow a subprogram specification. Annotations of subprogram declarations include constraints on formal parameters, results of subprogram calls, and conditions under which exceptions are propagated. The meaning of subprogram annotations in general is explained in this section. Further details concerning the different kinds of subprogram annotations are given in Section 6.2 for object annotations, in Section 6.5 for result annotations, and in Section 11.4 for propagation annotations.

```
subprogram_declaration ::=
    [ context_annotation ]
    ... ada_subprogram_specification ... ;
    [ subprogram_annotation ]

subprogram_specification ::=
    [ context_annotation ]
    ... ada_subprogram_specification ...
    [ subprogram_annotation ]

subprogram_annotation ::=
    where
        basic_annotation_list
```

A subprogram annotation consists of the reserved word **where** and one or more basic annotations separated by commas; it must appear immediately after the subprogram declaration and is said to annotate that declaration. The scope of a subprogram annotation is the same as for the subprogram declaration it annotates. In Anna, visibility of formal parameters of a subprogram declaration is extended so that they are directly visible in a subprogram annotation of that subprogram (see 8.3). Similarly, generic formal parameters of a subprogram are also visible in a subprogram annotation (see 12.1).

Subprogram annotations are elaborated upon each call to the subprogram, according to the rules given in the relevant sections for the different kinds of basic annotations. All occurrences of formal parameters with mode **in** (which include all parameters of a function) in a subprogram annotation are treated as if explicitly modified by **in**.

The meaning of a subprogram annotation is that it must be true of every call to the subprogram and that it acts as a declarative constraint over the subprogram body, i.e. with respect to the body of the subprogram it has the same semantics as an identical list of basic annotations placed at the beginning of the declarative part of the body.

The transformation of a subprogram annotation into the Anna Kernel is as follows. A subprogram annotation is equivalent to a set of identical basic annotations in the declarative part of the subprogram body, and a set of statement annotations of each call to the subprogram. For a procedure, the statement annotations annotate the procedure call; for a function, they annotate an assignment of the function call to an auxiliary variable. An object constraint in a subprogram annotation is transformed into both an in annotation and an out annotation of the call. A result annotation of a function is transformed into an assertion on the auxiliary variable. In the annotation of the subprogram call, occurrences of formal parameters in the basic annotations are replaced by the corresponding actual parameters. It is assumed that actual expressions with side effects have been removed from the call by prior assignments to auxiliary variables.

*Examples of annotations of subprogram declarations:*

```
      procedure RIGHT_INDENT(MARGIN : out LINE_POSITION);
--|       where out (1 ≤ MARGIN ≤ 120);
--        An out annotation, see 3.2.

      function "/" (NUMERATOR, DENOMINATOR : INTEGER) return INTEGER;
--|       where  DENOMINATOR ≠ 0;
--        The actual value of DENOMINATOR has to be different from 0. DENOMINATOR need
--        not be modified by in as it is an in parameter; see 6.2.

      procedure INCREMENT(X : in out INTEGER);
--|       where
--|           - 2 ** 36 < X < 2 ** 36,
--        A constraint annotation that must hold during execution of the body.
--|           out (X = in X + 1);
--        An out annotation.

      function COMMON_PRIME(M, N : INTEGER) return NATURAL;
--|       where return P : NATURAL =>
--|           IS_PRIME(P) and M mod P = 0 and N mod P = 0;
--        A result annotation; see 6.5.

      procedure PUSH(E : in ELEM);
--|       where
--|           STACK.LENGTH = SIZE => raise OVERFLOW;
--        A propagation annotation; see 11.4.
```

*Notes:*

In proofs of consistency of subprogram bodies and subprogram calls, subprogram annotations act both as constraints and as promises, in the following way: in annotations on parameters constrain any call and can be assumed in the subprogram body; out annotations and result annotations constrain the body (by constraining the final state or the value returned in the final state) and can be assumed in the calling program on returning from a call.

In transforming subprogram annotations for consistency checking at runtime it is obviously not necessary to distribute the basic annotations both as statement annotations of each call and as declarative annotations in the subprogram body; it suffices to perform checking in the body only.

## 6.2 ANNOTATION OF FORMAL PARAMETERS

Annotations constraining parameter values are expressed by object annotations as part of a subprogram annotation.

For a formal **in** or **in out** parameter X of a scalar type, X'DEFINED is assumed to be true throughout the subprogram body since Ada requires that the value of an actual scalar parameter with mode **in** or **in out** be defined. For a formal **out** parameter X of scalar type the value of the attribute X'DEFINED is assumed to be FALSE at the beginning of the body. Note that for formal **in** or **in out** parameters of composite types, Ada does not require that they be fully defined; for instance, for an array **in** parameter A, the attribute A'DEFINED may be false.

A constraint C(X) on an **in** parameter is equivalent to the constraint C(**in** X).

As with declarative out annotations, an out annotation of a subprogram needs to be satisfied only upon normal return from a subprogram call; it does not apply to exceptional termination of the subprogram body. Propagation annotations (see 11.4) may be used to annotate final values of subprogram parameters on abnormal termination.

Objects declared globally to a subprogram declaration or body are treated as if they were additional parameters: constants correspond to additional **in** parameters and variables to additional **in out** parameters, except that the value of a global variable is not necessarily defined. See also 6.3 for annotation of globals in subprograms.

*Examples of formal parameter annotations:*

```
    procedure EXCHANGE(OLD, NEW : in INDEX);
--|     where  OLD < NEW;
--      Since OLD and NEW are in parameters, this annotation is equivalent to
--      in OLD < in NEW;

    procedure P(X : in INTEGER;  Y, Z : in out INTEGER);
--|     where
--|         X > 0,
--|         Y ≤ Z;
--      Here X > 0 and Y ≤ Z must hold throughout the body and imply the assertions
--      in X > 0 and in ≤ in Z on entry and out Y ≤ out Z on exit.
```

*Notes:*

In addition to explicit parameter constraints stated in a subprogram annotation, a formal parameter is also constrained by an annotation of its subtype (see 3.3).

For an **in out** parameter X, the annotation

```
    out (X = in X);
```

means that the value upon exit is the same as the value upon entry, whereas,

```
    X = in X;
```

means that throughout the subprogram body each value of X is the same as the value upon entry, i.e., the value of X remains constant throughout.

For an **out** parameter X, an occurrence of **in** X in a subprogram annotation has an undefined value (as a consequence of Ada semantics), except for discriminants of records and array attributes (which may be defined).

## 6.3 ANNOTATIONS OF SUBPROGRAM BODIES

For a subprogram body, the semantics of a subprogram annotation following the subprogram specification part of the body before the reserved word, **is**, are the same as for an annotation of a subprogram declaration (see 6.1).

If a subprogram declaration and its body or stub occur in the same declarative part, the annotations of the specification parts of both must conform (see [Ada83, 6.3.1]). If the body or stub appears in a package body, the two sets of annotations must be consistent in the sense of Section 7.9.

Ada does not permit reading the value of an out parameter (except for certain constraint values). Accordingly, annotations in the subprogram body may not refer to an out parameter, unless they apply only to the final state associated with the body.

For a virtual Ada subprogram declaration, a body need not be supplied.

*Example of an annotation of a subprogram body:*

```
    procedure SWAP(U, V : in out ELEM)
--|     where
--|             out (U = in V and V = in U);
    is
        T : ELEM := U;
    begin
        U := V; V := T;
    end SWAP;
```

*Note:* As a consequence of the rule that, in general, a subprogram annotation of a subprogram body must be the same as that of the corresponding declaration, it is not possible to specify the effect of a subprogram on globals that are declared between the subprogram declaration and the body. If such effects are to be specified in the subprogram annotations, the declarations have to be reordered so that the global objects are visible at the place of the subprogram declaration.

## 6.4 ANNOTATIONS OF SUBPROGRAM CALLS

Annotations of subprogram calls are a special case of statement annotations. A subprogram call, like any simple statement, is considered to be an atomic operation. Thus, the values of an actual **in out** parameter on entry to and exit from a call can be constrained by an annotation of the call; its values during execution cannot be constrained by an annotation of the call, only by an annotation of the subprogram itself.

An actual **in out** or **out** parameter of a subprogram call in virtual Ada text is not permitted to be a variable nor a subprogram parameter of the actual Ada text. A call to a subprogram that might change an actual global variable is not allowed in virtual Ada text.

*Examples of annotations on subprogram calls:*

```
    SWAP(A, B);        --| out (A = in B and B = in A);
--  Constraint on a call imposed by the previous annotation on the body of SWAP

    INCREMENT (A);   --| - 2 ** 36 < A < 2 ** 36;  out (A = in A + 1);
--  Constraint imposed by the previous annotation of the specification of INCREMENT
```

*Note:*

Annotations of subprogram declarations imply constraints on the in and out values of actual parameters of calls (see 6.1 and 6.2). The actual constraint on a call is obtained by substituting the actual parameters of the call for the formals in the subprogram annotation.


## 6.5 RESULT ANNOTATIONS OF FUNCTION SUBPROGRAMS

A result annotation specifies the result of a function.

```
    result_annotation ::=
        return [identifier : type_mark =>] compound_expression
```

A result annotation starts with the reserved word **return**. The identifier is a logical variable; its scope extends from its first occurrence to the end of the result annotation; it is visible only in the compound expression. The type mark must be the same as that given for the result in the function specification. The only objects that a result annotation in a subprogram annotation may refer to are formal parameters of the function and global objects.

The meaning of a result annotation in a subprogram annotation is that it is a constraint on the value returned by the function: the value returned by the function when its computation is completed must satisfy any result annotation of the function. For a result annotation of the form, **return expression**, the value of the expression must be equal to the result. For a result annotation of the form, **return** identifier : type_mark => expression, any value that satisfies the expression is admissible as the result.

A result annotation may also be used as a declarative or statement annotation. In those cases it constrains the value returned by any return statement within its scope.

*Examples of result annotations in subprogram annotations:*

```
     function SQUARE(N : INTEGER) return INTEGER;
--|      where return N * N;

     function SQRT(N : NATURAL) return NATURAL;
--|      where
--|          return S : NATURAL => S ** 2 ≤ N < (S + 1) ** 2;
--       The result of SQRT is a solution of the expression following =>.

     function COMMON_PRIME(M, N : INTEGER) return NATURAL;
--|      where return P : NATURAL =>
--|          IS_PRIME(P) and M mod P = 0 and N mod P = 0;
--       The value returned by a call COMMON_PRIME(M,N) may be any natural number
--       that is a common prime factor of M and N.
```

## 6.6 OVERLOADING OF SUBPROGRAMS IN ANNOTATIONS

Overloading of a subprogram (actual or virtual) by a virtual subprogram specification for use in annotations and virtual text is achieved by a virtual subprogram specification satisfying the Ada overloading rules. However, this is subject to the restriction that a virtual declaration may not hide an actual declaration of the same identifier (see 1.1, 8.3).

## 6.7 OVERLOADING OF OPERATORS

The Anna rules for overloading the equality operator on limited types are given in 7.4.4. These impose restrictions on the usual Ada rules.

## 6.8 ATTRIBUTES OF SUBPROGRAMS

Anna introduces function attributes of subprograms in order to permit construction of expressions involving subprogram calls that would otherwise be illegal.

For every procedure P, the following function attribute is defined:

P'OUT            denotes a function that for given in values of the parameters of P returns a record whose components are the out values of the in out and out parameters of P. These values can be selected using the names of the formal parameters of P. The formal parameters to P'OUT are the same as those of P, where the modes are replaced by in. Those parameters of P that had mode out are treated as having default values in P'OUT.

For every visible subprogram P of a package S, the following function attribute is defined:

P'NEW_STATE    denotes a function that expresses the transformation of the package state
               associated with P (see 7.7); it returns a value of type S'TYPE. The formal parameters
               to P'NEW_STATE are the same as those of P, where the modes are replaced by **in**.
               Out parameters of P are treated as having default values in P'NEW_STATE. If the
               new state of package S upon normal completion of the call S.P is ST, then the
               function call, S.P'NEW_STATE, returns the value ST; otherwise it is undefined.

With respect to scope and visibility, a function attribute is treated as if it was declared immediately
following the specification of the corresponding subprogram. The attribute designator NEW_STATE
may be omitted in certain names denoting successor states (see 7.7.3). The defaults of those
parameters of the function attributes that correspond to **out** parameters of the subprogram are not
specified.

*Examples of expressions using the OUT attribute to denote out parameter values:*

```
     procedure POP(E : out ITEM);
        . . .

     POP'OUT(E => X).E                 --   The value of the actual parameter X on exit from POP.

     SWAP'OUT(R, S)                    --   Means the record aggregate (in S, in R).
     SWAP'OUT(U => R, V => S).U --        Means out value of U, i.e., in S (see 6.3).
     SWAP'OUT(U => 3, V => 5).U --        value = 5

     procedure BINARY_SEARCH(X : ORDERED_ARRAY; K : KEY; R : out INDEX);
        . . .
--| A(BINARY_SEARCH'OUT(X => A, K => 10, R => PLACE).R) = 10;
--       The index expression has the value of PLACE after the call
--       BINARY_SEARCH'OUT(A, 10, PLACE).
```

*Examples of NEW_STATE and OUT attributes.*

```
     STACK[PUSH'NEW_STATE(X)]
--       A state of the STACK package after executing a PUSH operation.

     STACK[PUSH'NEW_STATE(X)].POP'OUT(E => Y).E = X;
--       or, equivalently,
     STACK[PUSH(X)].POP'OUT.E = X;
--       The out value of Y after applying POP(Y) to a successor state
--       STACK[PUSH'NEW_STATE(X)] is denoted by the left side expression (see 7.7.3 and 7.9).
```

*Notes:*

It is recommended to write calls to OUT functions using the named parameter form of parameter
association to increase readability, especially when formal parameters names are used to select
components of the returned record value.

The actual parameter of the OUT function for a parameter of mode **in out** denotes the in value of the parameter association and can be an expression (in contrast to the actual parameter of the procedure in Ada, which must be a variable).

The inclusion of **in** parameters of OUT and NEW_STATE functions corresponding to **out** parameters of the subprograms makes it possible to handle the (rare) case where the constraint of an actual composite parameter in that position is used by the subprogram. This may be relevant for composite types; for instance, the discriminant of a variant record or the bounds of an array passed as an actual parameter of mode **out** may be accessed by the procedure. Since these parameters have default values, they may be omitted from calls to the OUT and NEW_STATE functions.

# 7. PACKAGE ANNOTATIONS

In this chapter annotation concepts are introduced to permit adequate annotation of packages and of programs that use packages.

The basic concept used in annotations of the visible part of a package or of a program using a package is the *package state*. Viewed from the outside, a package is treated conceptually as an object of some new type (not defined in Ada). The values of this type are called *states*. In Anna, package states are denoted by names and by sequences of operations. For each package the *type* of its states and the values of its *initial state* and *current state* can be denoted by attributes of that package.

A second fundamental concept is the *package axiom*. Axioms are annotations within the visible part after the reserved word **axiom**. They express properties of the visible items of a package that are guaranteed by the implementation in the package body. Axioms behave as promises outside of a package and may be assumed by all programs using the package. The package body is constrained by the axioms; that is, the implementation of the package must satisfy the package axioms.

## 7.1 PACKAGE STRUCTURE

```
package_specification ::=
    [ context_annotation ]
    ... ada_package_specification ...

package_body ::=
    [ context_annotation ]
    ... ada_package_body ...
```

Package annotations may appear in the specification and in the body of a package. For the purposes of annotation, the private part of a package should be considered to be part of the package body. We refer to both parts together as the *hidden part*. However, Anna maintains the Ada package structure; annotations may appear separately in both parts. Annotations in the visible part of a package specification are called *visible annotations*; annotations in the private part or body are called *hidden annotations*.

In general, the information contained in the Ada package specification is only sufficient for correct syntactic use of the package. The purpose of visible annotations is to describe the semantics of a package. The information conveyed by the visible annotation should be sufficient to understand the package and to make it unnecessary for a user to inspect the implementation in the private part and body. Visible annotations of a package specification have many possible uses. Firstly, they can be used in determining correct interfacing either during bottom up program development when the implementation of a package should be concealed, or during top down development when an implementation is not yet available. Secondly, during top down development, visible annotations defining the desired properties of a package provide a guide for the implementor; the package body must satisfy the visible annotations. Thirdly, visible annotations provide information that may be used to document and classify the package (in a database say) independently of any implementation.

Hidden annotations have two purposes: description of the intended behavior of the implementation of the package, and definition of a representation of all concepts used in the visible annotations in terms of the local items in the private part and body.

For a virtual Ada package declaration, a private part or body need not be supplied.

The body of any actual Ada program unit that is declared in a package visible part must appear in the declarative part of the package body. In the case of a virtual subprogram declared in a package visible part, a virtual body may be omitted: if a corresponding virtual body stub is provided in the body of the package, the separate virtual body may be omitted. Hidden annotations may be given for the virtual body stubs even though bodies need not be supplied (see 3.9).

*Notes:*

Hidden annotations of virtual units whose bodies are omitted (i.e., annotations of the corresponding virtual body stubs) provide basic assumptions for formal proofs of consistency between the visible and hidden parts of an Anna package (see 7.9).


## 7.2 VISIBLE ANNOTATIONS IN PACKAGE SPECIFICATIONS

Annotations in the visible part of a package specification are called *visible annotations.* They are declarative annotations; their scope is the same as the scope of an Ada declaration at the same position within the package specification. Visible annotations are constraints over their scope except in the case where they are axioms of the package (see 7.8).

Annotations in a package declaration are elaborated as part of the elaboration of the package declaration according to the rules for each kind of annotation.

Annotations on any entity declared in a package specification are part of the package annotation. All kinds of annotations may appear in the package visible part. In addition, the visible annotations of a package include axiomatic annotations (see 7.8).

An annotation of an individual entity declared in the package specification has the same meaning in its scope as any annotation of the same kind of declaration elsewhere, i.e., it has the meaning that would result if the package specification boundary was deleted and the entity was given a new unique name if necessary.

In object, subtype, and axiomatic annotations in the visible part of a package, the modifier **in** designates values at the point of elaboration of the annotation (as part of the package elaboration); in object annotations, **out** designates values upon exit from the declarative region immediately enclosing the package declaration. In visible subprogram annotations, **in** and **out** have their usual meaning (see 6.2).

An object annotation in the visible part of a package specification may not contain a variable declared outside of the package unless the variable is modified by **in**. This also excludes unmodified use of collections associated with outside access types and current states (see 7.7.2) of outside packages.

Conditions for visible annotations to be consistent with implementations of the visible entities in the hidden part are described in Section 7.9.

*Example of a package declaration with visible annotations.*

```
    package COUNTERS is

        type COUNTER is limited private;

--:     function VALUE(C : COUNTER) return NATURAL;

        procedure INITIALIZE(C : COUNTER);
--|         where out (VALUE(C) = 0);

        procedure INCREMENT(C : in out COUNTER);
--|         where out (VALUE(C) = VALUE(in C) + 1);

    private
        . . .
    end COUNTERS;
```

*Notes on the example:*

COUNTERS is specified in terms of a virtual mapping, VALUE, from values of type COUNTER into the natural numbers. Any implementation is correct if there is a definition of VALUE so that the annotations of INITIALIZE and INCREMENT are satisfied. Note that VALUE is not required to be one — one.

In order to construct annotations expressing visible properties, it is often necessary to introduce auxiliary operations by means of virtual declarations, such as VALUE.

*Notes:*

Visible annotations will normally refer to package states, in particular, successor states resulting from sequences of package operations. Such annotations provide a very powerful means of expressing properties of groups of visible entities in the package specification (see 7.7).

Visible package annotations are intended to specify properties of entities declared within the package. They may not constrain entities declared outside of the package.

## 7.2.1 Annotations of a Visible Type

A type declared in the visible part of a package may be annotated by a subtype annotation, which may be unmodified or modified (see 3.3). If the annotation is an unmodified subtype annotation it has the semantics as defined in Section 3.3 and, for private types, in Section 7.4.

The set of values of a (sub)type defined by a modified subtype annotation is the same as for the unmodified annotation. However, a modified subtype annotation only constrains objects declared outside the package body. Moreover, the constraint does not apply during execution of a subprogram of the package or the sequence of statements of the package body; it need only be satisfied upon entry to and normal exit from a visible subprogram, and on normal exit from the sequence of statements of the body. A modified type annotation has the same meaning as the unmodified annotation during execution outside the package body.

If the visible type is a private type, a modified subtype annotation on the full declaration can be given in the private part (see 7.4). In this case, the subtype annotation is not visible in the enclosing scope. In order to ensure that the constraint is satisfied by objects declared outside the package body it is sufficient to require that the constraint be satisfied by the objects only on entering and exiting the package.

For runtime checking, if a modified (sub)type annotation is visible then the transformation into the Anna Kernel for unmodified (sub)type annotations is applied outside the package body (see 3.3); that is, the annotation is distributed as a declarative object constraint over all declarations of objects of that type, as an object constraint in a subprogram annotation over formal parameters of subprograms declared outside the package, as **in** and **out** annotations over formal parameters of visible subprograms of the package, and as a result annotation of outside and visible functions returning values of the type. The constraint is also added as **out** annotations of the package body for each variable declared outside the body whose value may be changed by the sequence of statements of the body.

If the modified (sub)type annotation is a hidden annotation on the full declaration of a private type, then it is only transformed into **in** and **out** annotations of each body of a visible subprogram for each formal parameter of that type, as a result annotation, and also as an **out** annotation of the package body for each outside variable of that private type whose value may be changed by the sequence of statements of the body.

*Notes:*

It is expected that modified subtype annotations will be used primarily to annotate private types; see Section 7.4 for examples of such annotations. They permit efficient updating of values subject to Anna constraints.

During execution of a subprogram of the package, outside objects (including parameters of subprogram calls) may be assigned values from the base or parent type that do not satisfy a modified constraint. However, modified subtype annotations are checked when a visible subprogram is called from inside the package body. Therefore these objects must satisfy the constraint at internal calls as well as upon normal termination of a call from outside the package.

Variables of a type with a modified annotation that are declared within the body of the same package as the type are not constrained by that annotation.


## 7.3 HIDDEN PACKAGE ANNOTATIONS

Hidden annotations of a package consist of the annotations in the private part and body. Hidden annotations have two purposes:

- to specify the intended behavior of the implementation of the package. For this purpose annotations of objects, types, statements, subprograms, and packages are used to specify all entities declared within the body. These entities include both the bodies of actual program units declared in the visible part of the package and entities that are locally declared in the hidden part.

- to specify the implementation of all virtual entities declared in the visible part of the package.

*Example of annotation of the RATIONAL NUMBERS package body [Ada83, 7.3]:*

```
package RATIONAL_NUMBERS is
    type RATIONAL is
        record
            NUMERATOR    : INTEGER;
            DENOMINATOR  : POSITIVE;
        end record;

    function EQUAL(X, Y : RATIONAL) return BOOLEAN;
        ...
end;

package body RATIONAL_NUMBERS is

    procedure SAME_DENOMINATOR(X, Y : in out RATIONAL)
--|     where out (X.DENOMINATOR = Y.DENOMINATOR and
--|         EQUAL(X, in X) and EQUAL(Y, in Y) );
    is
        ...
    end SAME_DENOMINATOR;

    function EQUAL(X, Y : RATIONAL) return BOOLEAN
--|     where return
--|         X.NUMERATOR * Y.DENOMINATOR = Y.NUMERATOR * X.DENOMINATOR;
    is
        ...
    end EQUAL;
    ...

end RATIONAL_NUMBERS;
```

*Example of an annotated virtual declaration in the body of a STACK package:*

```
--: function LENGTH return INTEGER;
--|     where return INDEX;
--  LENGTH is a virtual function used in visible annotations of STACK. This specification
--  with annotation is declared in the body of STACK where the local variable INDEX is visible.
```

*Note:*

Hidden annotations of the body of a visible program unit are given in terms of full declarations of private types and the local objects of the hidden part. Therefore these hidden annotations are not merely a repetition of the visible annotations of the corresponding specification. Consistency of the package visible part with the body requires that both visible and hidden annotations are consistent with the body (see 7.9).

## 7.4 ANNOTATIONS ON PRIVATE TYPES

A private type declaration may be annotated by a subtype annotation as with any other type declaration. However, since a private type declaration in the visible part has no structure except for optional discriminants and default values (and the operations on the private type are declared later in the package specification so that they are not visible at that point) an annotation of a private type in the visible part is essentially trivial. In general, those properties of (the values of) a private type that can be described in the visible part of a package are expressed by annotations of the visible subprogram declarations and by axiomatic annotations.

Package axioms can be used to define the properties of the allowable (visible) operations on a private type by algebraic methods. Thus the Ada package and private type constructs together with the Anna package axioms provide a powerful method of defining abstract data types independently of any implementation.

An unmodified subtype annotation on the full declaration of a private type given in the private part applies in its immediate scope, i.e., from its position to the end of the package body. It has the normal semantics of a type annotation (see 3.3). It constrains all values assigned to objects of the type within the hidden part of the package. As a consequence, parameter values and function results of the type must obey the constraint for all subprograms whose bodies are in the package body. Since values assigned to variables of the private type declared outside the package can only be constructed by calling the visible subprograms of the package, it follows that the values of outside variables will also obey the hidden constraint. Thus it may always be assumed that if all previous calls to visible subprograms have terminated normally then the implemented (hidden) value of an outside variable obeys a constraint on the full declaration of a private type. This assumption is also valid when the subtype annotation is modified (see 7.2.1). Moreover, if the annotation is not modified, the assumption holds even in the case when calls to visible subprograms terminate exceptionally (see 6.4).

Subtypes of private types may be annotated in programs using a package. Such annotations can restrict the set of abstract (i.e., visible) values of the subtype of the private type in non-trivial ways since the package operations on the type are visible and can be mentioned in the annotation.

Annotations on a *limited private* type may use equality on that type since Anna defines a default equality operator for limited types (see 7.4.2).

*Example of a visible axiomatic annotation on a private type:*

```
package KEY_MANAGER is
     type KEY is private;
     NULL_KEY : constant KEY;
     procedure GET_KEY(K : out KEY);
     function "<" (X, Y : KEY) return BOOLEAN;
```

```
--|          axiom for all K : KEY => NULL_KEY < K or NULL_KEY = K;
             ...

      private
             type KEY is new INTEGER range 0 .. INTEGER'LAST;
             NULL_KEY : constant KEY := 0;

      end KEY_MANAGER;
--           NULL_KEY is the least ("<") member of the private type KEY;
--           A consequence of the axiom is that the procedure GET_KEY must satisfy
--           out (NULL_KEY < K or K = NULL_KEY).
```

*Example of a hidden annotation on a private type:*

```
      generic
             type ITEM is private;
             SIZE : POSITIVE;

      package ANY_QUEUE is

             type QUEUE is limited private;

             function    EMPTY  (Q : in QUEUE) return BOOLEAN;
             procedure   ADD    (X : in ITEM; Q : in out QUEUE);
             procedure   REMOVE (Q : in out QUEUE);
             function    FRONT  (Q : in QUEUE) return ITEM;
             ...

      private

             type TABLE is array (NATURAL range <>) of ITEM;
             type QUEUE is
                 record
                    STORE      : TABLE(0 .. SIZE - 1);
                    COUNT      : NATURAL range 0 .. SIZE     := 0;
                    IN_INDEX   : NATURAL range 0 .. SIZE - 1 := 0;
                    OUT_INDEX  : NATURAL range 0 .. SIZE - 1 := 0;
                 end record;
--|          where in out Q : QUEUE =>
--|              Q.IN_INDEX = (Q.OUT_INDEX + Q.COUNT) mod SIZE;

      end ANY_QUEUE;
```

```
--    A consequence of the semantics of modified type annotations (see 7.2.1) is that
--    the internal value of any variable of type QUEUE will obey the constraint
--    after normal termination of any call to an ANY_QUEUE operation on it.
```

*Example of an annotation on a subtype of a private type declared outside the package:*

```
      subtype PURE_IMAGINARY is COMPLEX_NUMBERS.COMPLEX;
--|          where Z : PURE_IMAGINARY => COMPLEX_NUMBERS.RE(Z) = 0.0;
--           The subtype PURE_IMAGINARY is declared in a program using the package
--           COMPLEX_NUMBERS (see 7.7).
```

*Note:*

As a consequence of the application of Ada rules to virtual text, a virtual visible private type declaration must have a virtual full declaration in the private part.


### 7.4.1 Use of Private Types in Annotations

The Ada restriction on the computational use of a private type within the specification part of the package that declares that private type applies also to annotations [Ada83, 7.4.1(4), 7.4.3(2)]; (see also 3.9). That is, names designating private types, subtype of private types, types that have subcomponents of private types, the package state type (see 7.7.1), and deferred constants may occur in annotations prior to the full declaration of those private types, provided elaboration of the annotations does not require computational use of those types and constants.

*Note:*

As a consequence of the rules of elaboration for subprogram annotations and axiomatic annotations, names of private types and deferred constants may occur in these kinds of annotations in the specification of the package declaring those private types.


### 7.4.2 Operations of a Private Type

The attributes DEFINED and INITIAL are available for a private type outside of the package declaring that type and in its specification part prior to the full declaration of the private type (see 3.3.3). The value of X'DEFINED for an object X of a private type is its value for the full declaration of the private type applied to the hidden value of X (see also 3.5, 3.6.2, 3.7.4, and 3.8.2). Similarly T'INITIAL denotes the default initial value of objects resulting from the full declaration of the private type T; it is undefined if there is no such value. Both attributes may not be used in an evaluation (see 3.9) before elaboration of the full declaration of the private type.

A default equality operator " = " is defined for limited private types. The default equality is the identity relation on the full declaration of the limited private type (see 4.5.2, 7.4.4).

Following Ada [Ada83, 7.4.2], the Anna operations that are implicitly associated with a private type as a consequence of its full declaration are available only in the hidden part of the package and after the full type declaration. For example, if a private type has a full declaration as an access type, the associated collection is available only in the hidden part.

*Note:*

The Anna type attributes, collection state type (3.8.2) and package state type (7.7.1), are treated like private types in Ada except that redefinition of the equality operator is allowed.

7.4.3             No additions

7.4.4 Redefinition of Equality for Limited Types

In Anna the equality operator " = " is predefined for all types including limited types (see 4.5.2, 7.4.2). The predefined equality on limited types is visible only in annotations and virtual text.

The equality operator " = " may be overloaded for limited private types (as in Ada) and also the Anna state type attributes. An overloaded equality operator must satisfy the restrictions stated below. Such an overloading hides the predefined Anna equality and therefore constitutes a redefinition.

A new (actual or virtual) specification of " = " for a limited private type (or Anna state type attribute) must appear in the visible part of the package declaring that limited private type. If the limited type is an actual type, the new declaration must be actual. At most one redefinition (actual or virtual) of an equality operator is permitted, and all occurrences of that operator must refer to the redefined meaning — i.e., the visible declaration must be placed before any use of the operator. Finally, the body of a function redefining equality may not refer to any object that is global to the body of the package in which that equality operator is declared.

A redefinition of " = " implicitly redefines "/ = " so that it is the complementary relation.

*Example of a redefinition of the predefined Anna equality on a limited private type.*

```
package SET_OF_STACKS is
    type STACK is limited private;
    function "=" (X, Y : STACK) return BOOLEAN;
        . . .
private
    type STACK is
        record
            SPACE : TABLE(1 .. SIZE);
            INDEX : NATURAL := 0;
        end record;
end SET_OF_STACKS;

package body SET_OF_STACKS is
        . . .
    function "=" (X, Y : STACK) return BOOLEAN
--|     where
--|         return X.INDEX = Y.INDEX and
--|             for all I : NATURAL range 1 .. X.INDEX =>
--|                 X.SPACE(I) = Y.SPACE(I);
    is
        . . .      -- body of "=".
    end "=";
        . . .
end SET_OF_STACKS;
--      Note the use of "=" on index and component types in annotating the new
--      meaning of "=" on the limited private type.
```

*Notes:*

The Anna restriction whereby a redefinition of " = " for a limited private type (or state type attribute) must be a visible (actual or virtual) function of the package declaring that type, implies that an equality operator is always required to satisfy the equality axioms (see 7.8.2). This would not be ensured unless the usual Ada rules for overloading " = " were restricted.

The Anna predefined " = " on a limited private type is defined as the identity relation on its full declaration and therefore coincides with the Ada predefined " = " on the full declaration when this is available.

Any redefinition of equality on a limited type is subject to the Anna restrictions whereby virtual subprograms may not hide actual subprograms. Redefinition of " = " on an actual limited private type must be actual to ensure that hiding of the Ada predefined equality on the full declaration by a virtual definition of " = " does not take place in the package body.

An Anna implementation may impose simple syntactic checks for reference to global objects in implementations of equality operators (see also 7.8.2).


**7.5 - 7.6**                       No additions


## 7.7 PACKAGE STATES

A basic new concept introduced in Anna for use in package annotations is the *package state*. This concept is intended to facilitate writing external annotations, i.e., visible package annotations that express properties of the visible items, and also annotations of programs that use the package.

Viewed from the outside, a package is a composite object of some new type (not defined in Ada). The values of this type are called *package states*. The type of the states is introduced as the TYPE attribute of a package. The structure of a package state is not visible from the outside. A state is composed of values of objects local to the package body; it does not include values of visible or global objects. Each package declaration (including generic instantiations) introduces a new state type associated with it.

After elaboration a package has an initial state. In Anna the initial state is denoted by the package attribute INITIAL.

Whenever a call on a visible procedure of a package (or function with side effects) is performed, a change in the package state may result. A state change can occur even if a subprogram call does not terminate normally (e.g. propagates an exception). States resulting from the execution of a sequence of subprogram calls, each of which terminates normally, are called *successor states*. Successor states are denoted by sequences of package operations and are names in Anna. The *current state* of a package at any point is denoted by the package attribute, STATE.

In general, a call to a visible subprogram of a package depends not only on the actual parameters, but also on the current state. Therefore the package state behaves as an additional parameter of the package subprograms.


**7.4 ANNOTATIONS ON PRIVATE TYPES**

### 7.7.1 State Types

The type of all states of a package P is denoted by the attribute P'TYPE. It is called the *state type* of P. Outside of P, P'TYPE has the same meaning in Anna as a limited private type declared at the beginning of the visible part of P. It is introduced as an attribute so that the virtual declaration is omitted. It may be used in annotations and virtual program text exactly as any other private type in Ada, except that in addition the predefined equality operator may be redefined (see 7.4.2). Its use is subject to restrictions similar to the Ada restrictions on the use of private types (see 7.4.1 and below).

Inside a package hidden part the state type has the meaning of a private type that has a virtual full declaration as a record type whose components are *all* the local variables of the package hidden part, all collections associated with local access types, and the current states of all local packages, in the order in which those entities are declared.

More precisely, let A : T1, B : T2, . . . be the local variables declared in the hidden declarative part of the package P. (That is, the private part and declarative part of the body are taken as a single declarative part called the hidden declarative part.) Let C, D, . . . be the access types, and let M, N, . . . be the nongeneric packages declared in the hidden declarative part of P. Then P'TYPE is treated as if in the hidden declarative part of P there is a type declaration of the form:

```
--:  type P'TYPE is
--:      record
--:          A : T1;
--:          B : T2;
--:          . . .
--:          C : C'COLLECTION'TYPE;
--:          D : D'COLLECTION'TYPE;
--:          . . .
--:          M : M'TYPE;
--:          N : N'TYPE;
--:          . . .
--:      end record;
```

If the variable declarations of A, B, . . . are constrained, then the record components are assumed to be similarly constrained. The *null* component list is assumed if the package does not have a body, or if its body does not contain any local variables, etc.

The rules for use of the state type are similar to those that apply to a private type (see 7.4.1). For the purpose of applying these rules, the implicit full record type declaration is assumed to be positioned in the hidden declarative part of the package (either in the private part or body) immediately after the last of the declarations of A, B, . . . C, D, . . . M, N, . . . , but before any of the bodies of the visible Ada subprograms. This imposes ordering requirements on the hidden declarative part. Most of these requirements are already imposed by Ada itself, and the only additional restriction is that local package declarations only appear as basic declarative items (see [Ada83, 3.9]). Use of the state type in annotations is no longer restricted from this position to the end of the package body. A type constraint on the state type may be placed at this position (see 7.7.5). However, the use of the state type in virtual Ada text is restricted; throughout the body of the package the only allowed occurrences of the state type name are in a subprogram specification or a entry declaration.

Assignment is a basic operation, and equality is a predefined operator, on package state types. Equality on state types is predefined as the identity relation. It may be redefined for a given package by giving a virtual declaration of the function " = " on the state type in the visible part and a body or body stub in the package body. For consistency, the redefined equality must satisfy the axioms for equality (see 7.8.2).

The Anna semantics of package state types within package bodies permits selection on states using the names of local objects, access types, and packages. Selected components of states may appear in expressions wherever the component names are visible. States may also be used as prefixes in expanded names.

*Examples of visible package annotations using state types:*

```
--| for all S1, S2 : RATIONAL_NUMBERS'TYPE; X, Y : RATIONAL =>
--|      S1.EQUAL(X, Y) = S2.EQUAL(X, Y);
--    The value of the function EQUAL on any two rationals is
--    independent of the state of the rational numbers package (see 7.3).

--| for all S : STACK'TYPE; X, Y : ITEM => S[PUSH(X); POP(Y)] = S;
--    For any state S of a STACK package, if a PUSH operation is performed
--    followed by a POP and both operations terminate normally, then the
--    resulting state is equal to S.

--: type STACK_STATE_HISTORY is
--:      record
--:            STATE : STACK'TYPE;
--:            NEXT  : POINTER;
--:      end record;
```

*Example of an implicit state type declaration:*

```
        package body KEY_MANAGER is

            LAST_KEY : KEY := 0;

--:         type KEY_MANAGER'TYPE is
--:             record
--:                 LAST_KEY : KEY;
--:             end record;

            procedure GET_KEY(K : out KEY)
--|             where out (LAST_KEY = in LAST_KEY + 1);
            is
                ...
            end GET_KEY;

            function "<" (X, Y : KEY) return BOOLEAN is
                ...
        end KEY_MANAGER;
```

*Examples of expressions involving internal state components:*

```
        KEY_MANAGER'INITIAL.LAST_KEY = 0
--              Internally, any state of the KEY_MANAGER package has a LAST_KEY
--              component; its initial value is 0 [Ada83, 7.4.2].
```

```
    for all S : KEY_MANAGER'TYPE; K : KEY =>
        S[GET_KEY(K)].LAST_KEY = S.LAST_KEY + 1;
--      Application of the procedure GET_KEY in any state of KEY_MANAGER
--      increments the LAST_KEY component of that state.
```

*Notes:*

An Anna package state does not contain components that are visible or global variables. Thus, for example, the collection of an access type declared outside the package hidden part is not a component of the package state. However, in general, the visiblity rules of Ada permit outside variables to be accessed in the body of a package. This means that values of such variables may influence the behavior of visible subprograms of the package. Dependencies on outside variables, i.e., variables that are not part of the Anna state of a package, should be avoided in an Ada package.

It may not be possible to formalize the behavior of a package that is dependent on outside variables since their values may be changed by operations that are not visible at the package declaration. Dependence on outside generic units or library units whose states are constant presents no problem.

The virtual record type defining the state type contains components corresponding to all virtual as well as actual local objects, collections of virtual as well as actual local access types, and states of virtual as well as actual local packages. A package state therefore embodies components whose values influence only virtual subprograms of the package, as well as components whose values can influence all subprograms.


### 7.7.2 Initial and Current States

The *initial* and *current* states of a package may be denoted by attributes of a package in Anna.

P'INITIAL denotes the *initial* state of a package P. The initial state is the state after elaboration of the body of P.

Use of the initial state attribute in annotations and virtual text is subject to the restrictions on the use of deferred constants (see 7.4.1). Thus the rules of use of the initial attribute are those that would apply to a deferred constant having a declaration at the beginning of the package specification and a full declaration at the end of the package body.

The attribute P'STATE denotes the *current state* of a package P. Its value is defined upon normal completion of the elaboration of the package body (it is then equal to the INITIAL attribute) and remains defined throughout a computation. Outside of the package, no structure of (the values of) the current state attribute is visible. The current state attribute can change value only as the result of a call to a visible subprogram of the package. Its value can change even if a subprogram call terminates exceptionally. Its value remains constant between calls. In the body of the package, it has as value the aggregate of values of the local variables, collections, and package states in any observable state. Thus for package P, the implemented value of P'STATE is (see 7.7.1):

```
    P'TYPE'(A, B, ..., C, D, ..., M, N, ...).
```

The current state attribute of a package P may not be used (in evaluations, as defined in 3.9) in annotations or virtual text until after elaboration of the body of P.

For notational convenience in annotations, the current state may be denoted by the package name itself; that is, the attribute designator STATE may be omitted.

The STATE attribute is a dynamic attribute of a package (see also collection attribute, 3.8.2). In annotations, it is treated as a program variable; its in value is used in the elaboration of a type annotation or axiom of another package, and its occurrences in annotations may be modified by in and out.

*Examples of initial states:*

```
KEY_MANAGER'INITIAL        --   Initial state of the KEY_MANAGER package.
INTEGER_STACK'INITIAL      --   Initial state of the INTEGER STACK package.
```

*Examples of current states:*

```
STANDARD'STATE             --   Current state of the package STANDARD,
STANDARD                   --   Current state of the package STANDARD,
INTEGER_STACK              --   Current state of the package INTEGER_STACK
```

*Example of an object constraint on a current state attribute:*

```
generic
      type ITEM is private;
      SIZE : NATURAL;
package STACK is

      OVERFLOW, UNDERFLOW : exception;

--:      function LENGTH return NATURAL;
         ...
end STACK;
         ...

package INTEGER_STACK is new STACK(ITEM => INTEGER, SIZE => MAX);
--|      INTEGER_STACK.LENGTH <= MAX - 1;
--       The values of INTEGER_STACK'STATE are constrained so that an OVERFLOW
--       exception will not occur in the using program.
```

*Notes:*

It should be emphasized that when the package name is used to denote the current state it is still an attribute and may not appear in virtual text on the left side of an assignment or as an out parameter of a procedure call.

Because P'STATE remains defined under exceptional termination of subprogram calls, it may be used to annotate conditions that must be satisfied when exceptions are propagated from packages (see 7.10, 11).

### 7.7.3 Successor Package States

A change in the state of a package may result from a call to a visible procedure or to a function with side effects. Those package states resulting from sequences of calls to visible subprograms of the package that complete normally are called *successor states* and are given a special notation in Anna by means of operation sequences.

```
package_state ::=
    state_name [ function_call {;function_call} ]
```

If the state name in a successor state is of type P'TYPE then the subsequent function calls must be to NEW_STATE function attributes of visible subprograms of P (see 6.8); the resulting name denotes a value of type P'TYPE.

The meaning of successor state names is defined as follows. Suppose A and B are visible subprograms of package P, and S is a state of type P'TYPE. Let P have state S as the result of starting in the initial state and executing a sequence of calls to visible subprograms, all of which completed normally. Then S[A'NEW_STATE(parameters)] designates the next state of P after normal completion of the call, P.A(parameters), and is undefined if this call does not complete normally.

Successor states with more than one function call are defined by,

```
S[A'NEW_STATE; B'NEW_STATE] = S[A'NEW_STATE][B'NEW_STATE]
```

For notational convenience in successor states, the attribute designator, NEW_STATE, may be omitted from function call terms placed inside the square brackets, and the names of the respective visible package subprograms may be used without the attribute designator. In addition, the names of visible subprograms may be used in successor states without the package name prefix since no ambiguity can result.

No method for runtime checking of annotations containing successor states is given in this document.

*Examples of successor states:*

```
ANY_QUEUE[ADD'NEW_STATE(A,Q1)][REMOVE'NEW_STATE(Q2)];
ANY_QUEUE[ADD'NEW_STATE(A,Q1); REMOVE'NEW_STATE(Q2)];
ANY_QUEUE[ADD(A,Q1); REMOVE(Q2)];
```
-- *Alternative notations for the successor state of the ANY_QUEUE package resulting*
-- *from the current state by executing calls to ADD and REMOVE.*

```
KEY_MANAGER'INITIAL[GET_KEY(A); GET_KEY(B)]
```
-- *The state of KEY_MANAGER after two calls to GET_KEY;internally this*
-- *state has the aggregate value, KEY_MANAGER'TYPE(LAST_KEY = > 2).*

```
STACK[PUSH(X); POP(Y)]
```
-- *A state resulting from the current state of STACK package after executing*
-- *a PUSH and a POP operation.*

*Notes:*

A successor state name denotes a state only under the assumption that all the calls to the NEW_STATE functions are defined. This implies that all associated subprogram calls leading to that state are completed, i.e., terminate and do not propagate exceptions; otherwise it is undefined (see 4.14).

At any point in a computation, if all subprogram calls to a package have completed normally, the successor state consisting of the initial state followed by the corresponding sequence of NEW_STATE function calls will be defined and equal to the current state.

Package axioms involving universal quantification over expressions containing successor states will generally be consistent with the underlying Ada text if they are consistent for those computations that do not propagate exceptions. This is a consequence of the semantics of universal quantification (see 4.11) and the rules for definedness of successor states.

The notation for states of arrays, records, and collections is a special case of the notation for states of packages.

### 7.7.4 Function Calls Relative to Package States

In general, values returned by calls to visible functions of a package depend on the state of the package. This state is the current package state, i.e., the state at the point of the computation where the call is made. Prefixing calls to package functions by states permits construction of expressions denoting values returned by function calls when the package is in the named state, not necessarily the current state. The package state in which a function call is to be executed is indicated by a package state prefix to the function call. Thus, if F is a visible function of package P and ST denotes a state of type P'TYPE, the expression ST.F(..) denotes the value returned by a call to F in state ST; the call to F is said to be *relative* to the package state ST. The state ST may be denoted by any name of the appropriate state type, in particular the initial and current states (see 7.7.2) and successor states (see 7.7.3). A call F( ... ) without a prefix denotes a call relative to the current state, P'STATE.F( ... ).

In a context where the function F is only visible by selection, the prefix denoting the package may be omitted from the function name, i.e. in place of ST.P.F(..) one may write ST.F(..). This shortens the notation without ambiguity since the package state prefix already provides the required information. This shortened notation is the preferred notation.

The package state denoted by the prefix of a function call is treated as an additional parameter of the function. Consequently, if the current state attribute appears in the prefix, then the current state of the package is a constituent variable of the expression containing the function call (see 1.2).

Note that the visible functions that can be called relative to a package state include the function attributes OUT and NEW_STATE of visible subprograms of the package (see 6.8).

*Examples of values resulting from subprogram calls relative to package states:*

        STACK[PUSH(A); PUSH(B)].LENGTH = STACK.LENGTH + 2
--      *Value returned by calling LENGTH in a state of the STACK package after two*
--      *calls to PUSH increases by 2 provided both calls terminate normally.*

```
    ST[PUSH(X)].POP'OUT(E => Y).E = X
--  The final value of the actual out parameter Y of a call to POP in state
--  ST[PUSH(X)] is X; E is the formal out parameter in the specification of POP.

    NULL_KEY < KEY_MANAGER.GET_KEY'OUT(K => A).K
--  NULL_KEY is < the value of the out parameter resulting from a call to GET_KEY
--  in the current state of the KEY_MANAGER package.
```

The notation for function calls relative to package states permits the use of Ada prefix notation for successor states in place of the square bracket notation. However, the attribute designator NEW_STATE may not be omitted if the prefix (or dot) notation is used for successor states (otherwise an ambiguity might arise). Thus,

```
    STACK'INITIAL[PUSH(X); POP(Y)]
```
and
```
    STACK'INITIAL.PUSH'NEW_STATE(X).POP'NEW_STATE(Y)
```

are two notations for the same successor state. The square bracket notation is the preferred notation for successor states.

*Note:*

It might appear that a function call STACK.LENGTH is ambiguous since the prefix STACK may be interpreted as either the package name prefix (i.e. part of the function name) or the name of the package state (denoting the current state). However, the value denoted under either interpretation is the same.

### 7.7.5 Annotations on State Types

Constraints on package state types may be given in Anna using subtype annotations (see 3.3). Such constraints provide a very important annotation facility.

```
state_type_annotation ::=
    subtype_annotation
```

A subtype annotation of a package state type may be placed in the body of the package. This takes the form of the usual subtype annotation except that the implicit type declaration for the state type is omitted. It must be placed in the hidden declarative part at the position of the implicit full state type declaration (see 7.7.1).

A subtype annotation on the implicit virtual full state type declaration has the usual meaning of a type constraint, i.e., it constrains the values of the state type from its position to the end of the package body. In particular it constrains all visible subprograms of the package since it is placed before any body of a visible subprogram. Also it constrains the current state attribute (see 7.7.2), and therefore constrains the aggregate of values of local objects. A unmodified constraint on this aggregate is often too restrictive on the implementation of the package body. A modified constraint on the state type may be given. A modified constraint will apply to the aggregate of local component values of the package state only on normal termination of calls to the visible subprograms of the package. Such a constraint has the same meaning as Hoare's concept of Monitor Invariant [9] and is a very powerful annotation technique.

*Example of a hidden subtype annotation on a state type:*

```
generic
    type ITEM is private;
    SIZE : POSITIVE;

package QUEUE is

    function    EMPTY return BOOLEAN;
    procedure ADD(X : in ITEM);
    procedure REMOVE;
    function    FRONT return ITEM;

    OVERFLOW, UNDERFLOW : exception;
end QUEUE;

package body QUEUE is

    type TABLE is array (NATURAL range <>) of ITEM;

    STORE       : TABLE(0 .. SIZE - 1);
    COUNT       : NATURAL range 0 .. SIZE := 0;
    IN_INDEX    : NATURAL range 0 .. SIZE - 1 := 0;
    OUT_INDEX   : NATURAL range 0 .. SIZE - 1 := 0;
--|    where in out Q : QUEUE'TYPE =>
--|        Q.IN_INDEX = (Q.OUT_INDEX + Q.COUNT) mod SIZE;

    function EMPTY return BOOLEAN is
    begin
        return COUNT = 0;
    end EMPTY;

    procedure ADD(X : ITEM) is
    begin
        if COUNT < SIZE then
            STORE(IN_INDEX) := X;
            IN_INDEX := (IN_INDEX + 1) mod SIZE; --   See note 2 below
            COUNT := COUNT + 1;
        else
            raise OVERFLOW;
        end if;
    end ADD;

    ...                             --   bodies of REMOVE and FRONT

end QUEUE;
```

*Notes on Example:*

1. The value of the state aggregate QUEUE'TYPE(STORE, COUNT, IN__INDEX, OUT_INDEX) upon exit from any of the QUEUE operations must satisfy the constraint; therefore the current state will also satisfy the constraint on entry to any operation provided previous operations have terminated normally.

7.7 PACKAGE STATES

2. Note that at this point the aggregate of local component values of the state would not satisfy the unmodified form of the constraint on QUEUE'TYPE. Also, if a numeric error is propagated during evaluation of the right hand expression, it will result in a state that does not satisfy the modified constraint.

3. The subtype annotation constrains QUEUE'TYPE. It has the semantics of the full virtual type declaration and a modified subtype annotation at the same position:

```
--: type QUEUE'TYPE is
--:      record
--:           STORE      : TABLE(0 .. SIZE - 1);
--:           COUNT      : NATURAL range 0 .. SIZE := 0;
--:           IN_INDEX   : NATURAL range 0 .. SIZE - 1 := 0;
--:           OUT_INDEX  : NATURAL range 0 .. SIZE - 1 := 0;
--:      end record;
--|      where in out Q : QUEUE'TYPE =>
--|           Q.IN_INDEX = (Q.OUT_INDEX + Q.COUNT) mod SIZE;
```

*Notes:*

In addition to a state type constraint, local component objects may be constrained individually. Constraints on local objects must hold throughout a package body. These constraints place stronger restrictions on individual components of the state than a modified state type annotation.


## 7.8 AXIOMATIC ANNOTATIONS

In Anna an axiomatic annotation may be given in a package visible part. An axiomatic annotation consists of one or more (usually quantified) compound expressions following the reserved word **axiom**.

```
axiomatic_annotation ::=
     axiom [quantifier domain {; domain} =>]
          boolean_compound_expression {, boolean_compound_expression} ;
```

In general, an axiomatic annotation will be a conjunction of universally quantified expressions, which are referred to as the *package axioms*. The syntax for axiomatic annotations permits individual conjuncts in the scope of a quantifier domain to be separated by commas instead of **and** operators. This use of "," is a shorthand for the conjunction of the expressions quantified individually. That is,

```
quantifier domain => A, B;
```

has the same meaning as

```
(quantifier domain => A) and (quantifier domain => B);
```

Note that this is *not* equivalent to

```
(quantifier domain => A and B);
```

in the presence of undefined expressions, as explained in 4.11.

An axiomatic annotation is elaborated by replacing all constituent program variables and attributes by their values. Thus program variables have the same meaning in package axioms as if they were modified by **in**. Elaboration of axioms does not replace deferred constants (of a private type declared in the same package specification) by their values. Thus, after elaboration, package axioms are closed quantified expressions not containing free program variables but possibly containing the names of deferred constants.

The meaning of package axioms is that (*i*) they are visible promises that may be assumed wherever the package specification is visible, and (*ii*) they are constraints on the hidden part of the package. As visible promises, package axioms express properties of the visible entities of the package that are promised to hold in the scope of its declaration. For example, in analyzing the correctness of a program that uses a package, the package axioms may be assumed. In the package hidden part each axiom corresponds to an annotation on the local entities. These hidden assertions may be constructed from the axioms according to rules given in the axiomatic semantics and described informally in Section 7.9. If the implementation satisfies the assertions then the axioms in the visible part of the package are consistent with the package body.

Package axioms are part of the Anna Kernel, but no method of runtime checking of package axioms is given in this document.

*Example of axiomatic annotations for an integer package*:

> *The predefined INTEGER type in STANDARD could be specified in Anna as follows:*

```
package INTEGERS is

     type INTEGER is  --   Implementation_defined;

--        The predefined operators:
          function "=" (LEFT, RIGHT : INTEGER) return BOOLEAN;
          function "+" (LEFT, RIGHT : INTEGER) return INTEGER;
          . . .

--|       axiom
--|          for all A, B, N : INTEGER =>
--|                A mod B = (A + N * B) mod B,
--|                A = (A / B) * B + (A rem B),
--|                (- A) / B = - (A / B),
--|                A / (-B) = - (A / B),
--|                A rem (-B) = A rem B,
--|                (- A) rem B = - (A rem B),
--|                . . . ;

     end INTEGERS;
```

*Notes on the example:*

A consequence of the universal quantifier in these axioms is that the axioms must hold only when the functional terms are defined. That is, if A and B are integers such that the expression $(A / B) * B + (A \text{ rem } B)$ is defined, then $A = (A / B) * B + (A \text{ rem } B)$ must be true; if the right side is undefined (say for a numeric error) then this particular instance of the axiom is not required to be true (see quantified expressions, 4.11).

**7.8 AXIOMATIC ANNOTATIONS**

*Example of axioms of a STACK package:*

```
    package STACK is
          . . .
--|       axiom
--|           for all ST : STACK'TYPE; X, Y : ELEM =>
--|               ST[PUSH(X); POP(Y)] = ST,
--|               STACK'INITIAL.LENGTH = 0, ...;
          . . .
    end STACK;
```

*Example of an axiomatization of a user-defined type:*

-- *REAL is some visible real type*

```
    package COMPLEX_NUMBERS is

        type COMPLEX is private;              --  User-defined type.
        I : constant COMPLEX;                 --  Deferred constant.

        function "+" (X, Y : COMPLEX) return COMPLEX;
        function "-" (X     : COMPLEX) return COMPLEX;
        function "-" (X, Y : COMPLEX) return COMPLEX;
        function "*" (X, Y : COMPLEX) return COMPLEX;
        function "/" (X, Y : COMPLEX) return COMPLEX;
        function MAKE_COMPLEX(X, Y : REAL) return COMPLEX;
        function RE(X : COMPLEX) return REAL;
        function IM(X : COMPLEX) return REAL;

--|     axiom                            -- Axiomatization of COMPLEX.
--|         for all  X, Y : COMPLEX =>
--|             I * I * X = - X,
--|             X  = MAKE_COMPLEX(RE(X), IM(X)),
--|             I  = MAKE_COMPLEX(0.0, 1.0),
--|             MAKE_COMPLEX(0.0, X) = I * MAKE_COMPLEX(X, 0.0),
--|             ...;
--          Note the use of the private type COMPLEX and the deferred constant I
--          in the axioms prior to their full declarations (see 7.4.1).
    private
        type COMPLEX is
            record
                RE : REAL;
                IM : REAL;
            end record;

        I : constant COMPLEX := (RE => 0.0, IM => 1.0);

    end COMPLEX_NUMBERS;
```

*Notes:*

Package axioms have the same rules of elaboration as subtype annotations (see 3.3).

The use of the reserved word **axiom** is crucial in designating the intended semantics of package axioms, namely that the boolean expressions following it may be assumed wherever the package declaration is visible, and also constrain the package body. If the word **axiom** is deleted the resulting boolean expression is simply a closed quantified object annotation which must be true at that position in order to be consistent with the package declaration.

Variables declared in the visible part of a package can be annotated as usual by object constraints. Axioms cannot be used to constrain the values of visible program variables; this is a consequence both of the rules of elaboration and of the semantics of axioms (whereby axioms are visible promises and not visible constraints).

If axioms are to be given for a user-defined type and associated operations, the type declaration must be encapsulated in a package. Generally this will be a private type declaration and the visible operations of the package will include the constructor and selector operations of the type.

The package STANDARD is treated specially in Ada; it forms a declarative region enclosing all library units. This means that axioms for STANDARD would not be visible to any program. This artificial situation could easily be remedied by restructuring STANDARD into a sequence of small logically meaningful packages of standard types, each with its own axioms, as in the example of the package INTEGERS.

### 7.8.1 Simplified Notation for Axioms

Calls to functions of a package are always taken relative to a package state (see 7.7.4). In all other kinds of annotations, the default package state for function calls (i.e. when no package state is explicitly given by a prefix) is the current package state. Package axioms are required to be closed quantified expressions (after elaboration). Since (unprefixed) function calls in axioms do not refer to any particular package state, the default state relative to which such function calls are evaluated has to be expressed as a universally quantified logical variable of the state type. This means that an axiom containing unprefixed function calls is equivalent to (i.e. has the same meaning as) the axiom that results from performing the following steps:

1. A new universal quantifier over the package state type containing a new logical variable, S say, that does not occur yet in the axiom is added as the outermost (i.e. leftmost) quantifier of the axiom.

2. Each call to a function of the package is prefixed by S; this may require a change from infix to prefix notation.

Omission of the leading universal quantifier and the corresponding prefixes simplifies axioms in many cases; in particular, it permits the use of infix notation for binary operators. For example, when the properties of a package are independent of its state — which is always true when the state is trivial, as in the package COMPLEX_NUMBERS — axioms specifying visible package entities may be given without reference to the state of the package. The simplified notation is the preferred notation when applicable.

*Example:*

In the axiomatic annotation of the package INTEGERS, the first axiom,

```
    axiom
        for all A, B, N : INTEGER =>
            A mod B = (A + N * B) mod B, ...
```

is equivalent to the fully prefixed axiom,

```
    axiom
        for all S : INTEGERS'TYPE; A, B, N : INTEGER =>
            S."=" (S.mod (A,B), S.mod (S."+" (A, S."*" (N,B)), B)), ...
```

7.8.2 Implicit Axioms for Equality

In Anna a predefined set of axioms must be satisfied by each explicitly defined equality operator " = " on a limited private type of a package, including the state type (see 7.7.1). The axioms are *(i)* the axioms of reflexivity, symmetry, and transitivity, *(ii)* the substitution axiom for each visible function (including virtual functions and function attributes), and *(iii)* the axiom of independence of the package state,

```
        for all S1, S2 : P'TYPE; X, Y : T =>
            S1."=" (X,Y) = S2."=" (X,Y);
```

These axioms are implicit axioms of the package in which the equality operator is redefined (see 7.4.4).

*Example of implicit equality axioms for SET_OF_STACKS:*

```
    package SET_OF_STACKS is

        type STACK is limited private;
--:     function   "=" (X, Y : STACK) return BOOLEAN;
        procedure PUSH(X    : ELEM; S : in out STACK);
        procedure POP (X    : out ELEM; S : in out STACK);
        function   TOP (S   : STACK) return ELEM;
        ...
--|     axiom
--|         for all U, V, W : STACK; E : ELEM =>
--|             U = U,                        --  Reflexivity
--|             U = V → V = U,                --  Symmetry
--|             U = V and V = W → U = W,      --  Transitivity
--          Substitution axiom for the function TOP:
--|             U = V → TOP(U) = TOP(V),
--          Substitution axioms for the OUT attributes:
--|             U = V → PUSH'OUT(X => E, S => U).S =
--|                         PUSH'OUT(X => E, S => V).S,
            ...
--          independence of the package state:
--|             for all ST1, ST2 : SET_OF_STACKS'TYPE =>
--|                 ST1."=" (U,V) = ST2."=" (U,V);

    end SET_OF_STACKS;
```

*Notes:*

Ada does not impose any semantic restrictions on an equality operator declared on a limited private type. Anna, on the other hand, requires that an overloaded " = " satisfies very strong conditions in order to guarantee that that function possesses the usual mathematical properties of equality. The conditions include independence from objects that are global to the package in which the equality is declared (see 7.4.4) as well as independence of the state of the package. The body of the function " = " may reference variables that are local to the package body.

Dependence on the state of a package, P, would imply that a call of the form, P . "="(A, B), where A and B are fixed values of the limited type, could have different results at different times.

All predefined " = " operators satisfy the Anna predefined axioms for equality; the requirements on equality are therefore only imposed when " = " is overloaded.

## 7.9 CONSISTENCY OF ANNA PACKAGES

In this section we give an informal outline of what must be done to establish the consistency of a package. The two methods, formal verification or runtime checking, may be applied. The axiomatic semantics of Anna packages are an area of current research. A previous study on proving the consistency of packages may be found in [13].

The alternative method of runtime consistency checking is applicable to a large extent; much of the package consistency problem can be reduced to checking other constructs, e.g., to checking subprogram annotations, type constraints, etc., as described in other chapters. But it should be noted that package axioms are part of the Anna Kernel (see 1.3.2). Therefore runtime checking of consistency of axiomatic annotations is not transformed to checking the consistency of assertions but must be checked directly. Since axioms are usually universally quantified expressions where the quantifiers range over large domains of values such as the states of the package, the standard method of checking quantified expressions (see 4.11) cannot be regarded as practical.

Consistency of an Anna package may be separated into two consistency problems: *(1)* consistency of the package body, and *(2)* consistency of the package visible part with the body.

Consistency of a package with annotations of basic declarations in the package visible part that are independent of the package body — e.g., an annotation of a (sub)type that is not private, or an object constraint — is established according to the method (proof or runtime checking) for that kind of annotation and is independent of the package.

### 7.9.1 Consistency of the Package Body

To establish consistency of an Anna package body, the private part and body are taken together as a single scope called the *hidden part*; all declarations in the private part are considered to be placed at the beginning of the declarative part of the body. Consistency of the body requires showing that type and object constraints are satisfied within the hidden part, subunits declared in hidden declarative part satisfy their annotations, and so on.

Any modified type constraint (e.g., on a private type or the state type) may be assumed to hold on entry to a visible subprogram for **in** and **in out** parameters of that type, and must be established for **in out** and **out** parameters and result values of the type upon exit from a subprogram (see 7.2.1). In particular, a modified state type constraint may be assumed for the current state aggregate on entry to a visible subprogram and must be satisfied by the current state on exit (see 7.7.5). For unmodified type constraints the normal rules apply (see 3.3); for example, the current state aggregate must satisfy an unmodified constraint on the state type throughout the body of the package.

*Note:*

If calls to visible subprograms of the package do not occur in its body then establishing consistency of the body with modified type constraints is much simplified. If a visible subprogram is called inside the package hidden part, it cannot be assumed that actual parameters of the call satisfy a modified constraint; this may make it more difficult to establish correctness of the call.

## 7.9.2 Consistency of Visible Annotations with the Package Body

Generally, a package visible part contains basic declarations of entities whose implementations (i.e., full declarations or bodies) appear in the hidden part. The visible annotations will contain references to these entities. The most important examples are annotations of subprogram specifications and axioms. In this case it must be shown that the visible and hidden parts are consistent.

Visible annotations are translated into equivalent hidden annotations, and these must then be shown consistent with the hidden part. For example, visible annotations of a subprogram specification are translated into hidden annotations of the corresponding subprogram body, which must then be shown to satisfy these annotations (in addition to any other annotations given in the body). Axioms, which are — usually quantified — boolean expressions not containing program variables after elaboration, are translated into hidden expressions without program variables. These expressions must be true — i.e., they must be provable from facts about the hidden part — in order to be consistent with the body. Full details on demonstrating consistency of visible annotations with package bodies are beyond the scope of this document. Here we give a brief outline of the translation of visible annotation and demonstration of their consistency, with examples to illustrate the main ideas.

The translation replaces visible expressions by their hidden implementations. For example, a deferred constant is replaced by its hidden value; an object of a private type (see 7.4.1) is replaced by a unique aggregate representing its internal value in the most general form; a successor state is replaced by a sequence of calls to the hidden subprograms whose function attributes (NEW – STATE attributes) appear in the state. The resulting translation of a visible annotation is a hidden annotation.

In establishing the consistency of the translated visible annotations with the hidden part, the annotations of the hidden part may be assumed since their consistency is established separately. These assumptions include, for example, annotations of all hidden subprogram bodies (both actual and virtual) and any hidden constraints on types. Assumption of hidden annotations may be used, to simplify the translated annotations by replacing subexpressions by their values, or to establish their consistency.

Note that definedness of a visible annotation must be taken into account in establishing consistency with the body (see 4.14 for definedness of expressions). However, since definedness usually involves termination of function calls, it is often not possible to represent the full actual condition to be established in Anna itself.

*Example of visible and hidden annotations (See also 7.10):*

```
      package STACK is
--:        function "=" (S, T : STACK'TYPE) return BOOLEAN;
--:        function LENGTH return NATURAL;

           procedure PUSH(X : in ITEM);
--|            where in STACK.LENGTH < SIZE,
--|                out (STACK.LENGTH = in STACK.LENGTH + 1);

           procedure POP(E : out ITEM);
               ...
--|        axiom for all S : STACK'TYPE; X, Y : ITEM =>
--|            S[PUSH(X); POP(Y)] = S;
               ...
      end STACK;

      package body STACK is

           type TABLE is array (POSITIVE RANGE <>) of ITEM;
           SPACE : TABLE(1 .. SIZE);
           INDEX : NATURAL range 0 .. SIZE := 0;

--:        function "=" (S, T : STACK'TYPE) return BOOLEAN;
--|            where return S.INDEX = T.INDEX and
--|                for all K : NATURAL range 1 .. S.INDEX =>
--|                    S.SPACE(K) = T.SPACE(K):

--:        function LENGTH return NATURAL;
--|            where return INDEX;

           procedure PUSH(X : in ITEM)
--|            where
--|                in INDEX < SIZE,
--|                out (SPACE = in SPACE[INDEX => X]),
--|                out (INDEX = in INDEX + 1);
           is
                   ...

           procedure POP(E : out ITEM)
--|            where
--|                in INDEX > 0,
--|                out (INDEX = in INDEX - 1 and
--|                    SPACE = in SPACE and
--|                    E = in SPACE (in INDEX));
           is
                   ...

      end STACK;
```

*Example: Consistency of a visible subprogram annotation.*

The visible annotations on PUSH in the STACK package,

```
in STACK.LENGTH < SIZE,
out (STACK.LENGTH = in STACK.LENGTH + 1);
```

are translated into equivalent hidden annotations by the following steps.

First, STACK, the visible name for the current state, is replaced by the aggregate that designates its hidden value, (SPACE, INDEX), of type STACK'TYPE. This leads to intermediate annotations involving the expression,

```
(SPACE, INDEX).LENGTH
```

which indicates a call to LENGTH to be evaluated in the context of the aggregate. (Note that the intermediate expression is not a legal Anna boolean expression until the call to LENGTH is replaced by its value.) The hidden annotation of LENGTH may now be used to replace the function call by its hidden value; this results in hidden annotations of the body of PUSH:

```
in INDEX < SIZE;
out (INDEX = in INDEX + 1);
```

When replacing the function call to LENGTH, its definedness must be considered; the call is defined when the value of the state aggregate is defined and satisfies any annotations for LENGTH, and the call terminates (see 4.14).

Consistency of these annotations with the body may be established directly by considering them as additional annotations of the body of PUSH, or by showing that it can be deduced from the hidden annotations of PUSH. In this example, the translated annotations are just a subset of the hidden annotations. In the general case, consistency of the translated annotations with the body can be deduced from the hidden annotations if the translated in annotations imply the hidden in annotations, and the hidden out annotations imply the translated out annotations. These implications must take definedness into account; implication means, for example, that whenever the translated in annotation is defined and its value is true, then the hidden in annotation is also defined and true.

*Example: Translation of a STACK axiom and its consistency with the body:*

The STACK axiom in the visible part above is translated into an equivalent hidden quantified expression. First, the successor states represented in the left hand side are given unique names:

```
U = S[PUSH(X)], V = U[POP(Y)]
```

so that the expression in the axiom may be rewritten as,

```
      for all S, U, V : STACK'TYPE; X, Y : ITEM =>
(1)       U = S[PUSH(X)] and V = U[POP(Y)] → V = S
```

In determining whether expression (1) is true, only those elements of the domains of quantification, i.e. states and items, need to be considered for which the expression following => is defined (see 4.11). We may thus add in (1) definedness premises for all states. Let DEF(E) represent the conditions for an expression E to be defined; DEF(U), for instance, translates into, "S and X satisfy the in annotations of PUSH, the call to PUSH terminates normally, and the state U satisfies the state type constraint and the out annotations of PUSH." (Here, both visible and hidden annotations of PUSH must be considered.) Expression (1) is thus equivalent to,

```
        for all S, U, V : STACK'TYPE; X, Y : ITEM =>
(2)         DEF(S) and DEF(U) and DEF(V) and then U = S[PUSH(X)]
            and V=U[POP(Y)] → V = S
```

For the sake of brevity, the universal quantifiers are omitted in the following translation steps.

Next, we replace each state name by a unique hidden aggregate value:

```
    S = (SPACE_0,INDEX_0),  U = (SPACE_1,INDEX_1),  V = (SPACE_2, INDEX_2)
```

The definedness premises of expression (2) are then expanded into expressions involving the hidden aggregate values, using the hidden annotations on PUSH and POP and constraints on the state type. For instance, DEF(U) is replaced by,

```
    INDEX_0 < SIZE and 0 ≤ INDEX_1 ≤ SIZE
    and SPACE_1 = SPACE_0[INDEX_0 + 1 => X] and INDEX_1 = INDEX_0 + 1
```

Similarly, the equations in (2) between S, U and V are transformed into equivalent hidden equations between the aggregates using the hidden annotation of the operator "=" on the state type. The resulting translation of the axiom is:

```
    for all SPACE_0, SPACE_1, SPACE_2 : TABLE(1 .. SIZE);
            INDEX_0, INDEX_1, INDEX_2 : NATURAL;
            X, Y : ITEM =>
        0 ≤ INDEX_0 ≤ SIZE and
        0 ≤ INDEX_1 ≤ SIZE and
        0 ≤ INDEX_2 ≤ SIZE and
        INDEX_0 < SIZE and
        SPACE_1 = SPACE_0[INDEX_0 + 1 =>  X] and
        INDEX_1 = INDEX_0 + 1 and
        INDEX_2 = INDEX_1 - 1 and
        SPACE_2 = SPACE_1

        → INDEX_2 = INDEX_0 and
          (for all K : NATURAL range 1 .. INDEX_0  =>
                   SPACE_2(K) = SPACE_0(K)).
```

This final translation of the axiom is easily seen to be true, thus establishing consistency of the axiom with the body of STACK.

*Notes:*

The implicit equality axioms for a package (see 7.8.2) must also be translated into hidden equivalents and proved.

At Step 1 (see 7.9.1) the actual package body is proved consistent with its annotations. At Step 2 (see 7.9.2) the hidden specifications of both actual and virtual subprograms may be *assumed* in translating visible annotations into equivalent hidden annotations and demonstrating consistency of the resulting annotations with the body. Because of Step 1, assumption of actual subprogram hidden specifications is consistent with the actual body. Therefore, Step 2 also establishes consistency between the actual body and the hidden specifications of visible virtual subprograms. For example, if " = " is specified as the identity relation on states, the previous demonstration of consistency of the STACK axiom would require a change in the **out** annotations for POP whereby the POP-ed component of SPACE is given back its initial value.

Virtual visible concepts are introduced solely to express the visible annotations. These concepts are *given*, i.e., must be *understood* prior to implementation of the body, otherwise an implementor will not understand the visible annotations that are to be implemented. In the package body, the definition of the virtual concepts is given. If such a definition is omitted, visible annotations cannot be translated into equivalent hidden annotations. It is for this reason that hidden specifications of visible virtual subprograms are required if no body is given; these specifications must be expressed in terms of hidden objects (see 7.1).

## 7.10 EXAMPLE OF A PACKAGE WITH ANNOTATIONS

This section contains a complete stack package with formal comments. Further examples of annotated complete packages are given in Appendix H.

*Example of a stack package*

The annotations of this version of a stack package differ from those used in the previous sections: The annotations of the procedures PUSH and POP contain propagation anotations instead of explicit **in** constraints on the package state. The effect of this change is that calls to the procedures in the exceptional situations will not be inconsistent, but will merely raise an exception that can then be handled in the calling scope.

```
        generic
            type ITEM is private;
            SIZE : NATURAL;
--|             SIZE > 0;           --   Constraint on generic parameter SIZE (see 12.1)
        package STACK is
            OVERFLOW, UNDERFLOW : exception;

--:         function LENGTH return NATURAL;
--          Virtual function declared for use in annotations.

--:         function "=" (S, T : STACK'TYPE) return BOOLEAN;
--          Equality on the state type is being redefined.

            procedure PUSH(E : in ITEM);
--|             where
--|                 in STACK.LENGTH = SIZE => raise OVERFLOW,
--|                 raise OVERFLOW => STACK = in STACK;
--              If overflow is propagated the current state will be equal to the input state.

            procedure POP(E : out ITEM);
--|             where
```

```
--|                     in STACK.LENGTH = 0 => raise UNDERFLOW,
--|                     raise UNDERFLOW => STACK = in STACK;

--|         axiom for all ST : STACK'TYPE; X, Y : ITEM =>
--|             ST[PUSH(X); POP(Y)] = ST,
--|             ST[PUSH(X)].POP'OUT(E => Y).E = X,
--|             STACK'INITIAL.LENGTH = 0,
--|             0 <= ST.LENGTH <= SIZE,
--|             ST[PUSH(X)].LENGTH = ST.LENGTH + 1,
--|             ST[POP(X)].LENGTH  = ST.LENGTH - 1;
```

--      *The axioms are consistent with the STACK body if they are consistent under*
--      *the assumption that no exceptions are propagated; otherwise the successor*
--      *states are undefined (7.7.3) and the universally quantified axioms are*
--      *then vacuously true.*

```
    end STACK;

    package body STACK is

            type TABLE is array (POSITIVE range <>) of ITEM;
            SPACE : TABLE(1 .. SIZE);
            INDEX : NATURAL range 0 .. SIZE := 0;

--:         function LENGTH return NATURAL;
--|             where return INDEX;
```

--      *Redefinition of " = " on STACK'TYPE.*

```
--:         function "=" (S, T : STACK'TYPE) return BOOLEAN;
--|             where return  S.INDEX = T.INDEX   and
--|                 (for all K : NATURAL range 1 .. S.INDEX =>
--|                     S.SPACE(K) = T.SPACE(K));

            procedure PUSH(E : in ITEM)
--|             where out (INDEX = in INDEX + 1 and
--|                 SPACE = in SPACE[INDEX => E]);
            is
            begin
                if INDEX = SIZE then
                    raise OVERFLOW;
                else
                    INDEX := INDEX + 1;
                    SPACE(INDEX) := E;
                end if;
            end PUSH;

            procedure POP(E : out ITEM)
--|             where out (INDEX = in INDEX - 1 and
--|                 SPACE = in SPACE and
--|                 E = SPACE (in INDEX));
            is
            begin
                if INDEX = 0 then
                    raise UNDERFLOW;
```

```
            else
                E := SPACE(INDEX);
                INDEX := INDEX - 1;
            end if;
        end POP;

    end STACK;
```

*Notes on the example:*

The implicit virtual full declaration of the STACK state type (see 7.7.1) is:

```
--: type STACK'TYPE is
--:     record
--:         SPACE : TABLE(1 .. SIZE);
--:         INDEX : NATURAL range 0 .. SIZE := 0;
--:     end record;
```

If INDEX was not constrained to be in the range 0 .. SIZE, a weaker constraint on the aggregate, STACK'TYPE'(SPACE, INDEX) which would hold on exit from the STACK operations could be stated by constraining the state type:

```
--|        where in out S : STACK'TYPE => 0 ≤ S.INDEX ≤ SIZE;
```

This constraint on STACK'TYPE is equivalent to a monitor invariant in Hoare's sense [9].

# 8. VISIBILITY RULES IN ANNOTATIONS

**8.1**                    No additions

## 8.2 SCOPE OF DECLARATIONS AND DECLARATIVE ANNOTATIONS

The scope rules for virtual Ada text are the same as for actual Ada text. For instance, the scope of a virtual declaration is the same as if the preceding comment indicator for virtual text is removed and the declaration is considered to be in the Ada text at the same point.

The scope of a basic annotation is the same as for an Ada declaration at that position. The scope of a subtype, subprogram or axiomatic annotation extends from the place of the annotation to the end of the scope of the (sub)type, subprogram, or package which it annotates.

The scope of a declaration in the domain of a quantified expression, result annotation or subtype annotation, i.e. the scope of a logical variable, extends from the declaration to the end of the expression or annotation.

*Note:*

The scope of a basic annotation in an inner declarative region is purely local. For example, the scope of an object annotation on a global variable only extends from the object annotation to the end of the declarative region in which it is *immediately* enclosed.

*Example:*

```
    declare
        X : INTEGER;
    begin
        . . .
        declare
--|         in X = X;
        begin
            . . .        --  Here X is constrained to be constant.
        end;
        . . .            --  Here X is not constrained.
    end;
```

## 8.3 VISIBILITY

Declarations are visible *by selection* at additional places that are defined as follows:

> A formal procedure parameter is visible in a named parameter association of a call to the associated function attribute, OUT; a formal **in out** or **out**

parameter is also visible as selector in a selected component whose prefix is
a call to the function attribute OUT.

An identifier declared in the domain of a quantified expression or a subtype or result annotation (i.e.,
a logical variable, see 1.2) is only visible in the boolean expression following the delimiter = >; there it
hides any other (logical or program) variable with the same name.

A virtual declaration is visible only in other formal comments (virtual text and annotations) within its
scope. A virtual declaration that hides an actual entity is not permitted (see 1.1).

Formal parameters are directly visible in a subprogram annotation that immediately follows the
subprogram specification in which they are declared.  Similarly, generic formals are visible in
subsequent annotations of generic parameters.

*Examples:*

```
    function IS_PRIME (X : INTEGER);
--|      return not exist Y, Z : NATURAL =>
--|          Y > 1 and Z > 1 and X = Y * Z;
--       The parameter X is visible in the subprogram annotation.

    declare
        X, Y : INTEGER;
    begin
        . . .
--|     for all Y : INTEGER => EVEN(Y) → X ≠ Y;
--      The outer Y is hidden by the logical variable Y in the boolean expression following =>.
        . . .
    end;
```

### 8.4            No additions

### 8.5 RENAMING DECLARATIONS

A renaming declaration introduces another name for an existing entity.  The properties of the entity
are not affected by renaming; accordingly, the constraints associated with the new name are exactly
those of the renamed entity.  Specifically, if Anna permits further annotation of the renamed entity,
(i.e., if the entity is an object) then it is not relevant which name for the entity is being used in an
additional annotation.

An (actual) Ada object that is renamed in virtual text remains an actual object, thus the usual
restrictions on its use in virtual text apply (see 1.1).

**8.6**          No additions


## 8.7 THE CONTEXT OF OVERLOAD RESOLUTION

In addition to the three complete contexts defined in Ada, an annotation is also a complete context for the purpose of overload resolution.

An annotation is legal if there is exactly one interpretation of each constitutent of the innermost complete context which satisfies the following constrant:

1. If the annotation is a result annotation with no logical variable, then there is exactly one interpretation.

2. In all other cases, there is exactly one interpretation such that the annotation yields a BOOLEAN value.

# 9. TASK ANNOTATIONS

*Omission:*

A theory of annotations of tasks and multitask systems has yet to be developed.  Extensions of Anna to tasks are planned.

# 10. PROGRAM STRUCTURE

## 10.1 ANNOTATIONS OF COMPILATION UNITS

```
context_clause ::=
    {with_clause {use_clause} [context_annotation]}

context_annotation ::=
    limited [to name {, name};]
```

### 10.1.1 Virtual Context Clauses

A virtual library unit can be made visible in virtual text by inclusion of a virtual context clause naming that unit.

*Note:*

As a consequence of the rules for making declarations directly visible by use clauses [Ada83, 8.4], a potentially visible declaration in a virtual library unit will not be made directly visible by a virtual use clause if this would result in hiding a declaration made in actual Ada text. The usual rules for uniqueness of names apply also to the identifiers of virtual library units.

### 10.1.2          No additions

### 10.1.3 Context Annotations

A context annotation constrains the use of variables that are global to a program unit. The scope of a context annotation is a program unit. It constrains the occurrences of variables declared outside of its scope: only those outside variables that are listed in the name list of the context annotation may occur within its scope. A program unit is consistent with a context annotation whose scope encloses it if all variables declared outside the scope and occurring in the unit are named in the context annotation. The meaning of a context annotation is thus the same as if the visibility of outside variables were restricted in the annotated unit.

A context annotation may be given as part of a context clause, in a declarative part, or in a subunit. A context annotation that follows a context clause may name only variables that are declared in the visible parts of library packages named in the context clause. A package name may be used in a context annotation as an abbreviation for the list of all variables that are declared in its visible part.

A context annotation that follows a context clause applies to the subsequent library unit and also to any secondary unit that defines a corresponding body. It constrains the use in that unit of variables from library packages made visible by the context clause to the variables in the name list. If the unit to which the context annotation applies is a secondary unit, then use of outside variables in the unit body is restricted to those named in the annotation or else in a context annotation that precedes the corresponding declaration (i.e. the annotations of a library unit and its body are additive).

A context annotation that appears in a declarative part must immediately precede the declaration or body of a program unit. If it precedes a declaration, its scope is the declarative region associated with that unit; it constrains the use within its scope of all variables that are declared outside. A declarative context annotation that precedes a body applies to that body. Use of outside variables in the body is restricted to those named in the annotation or else in a context annotation of the preceding corresponding declaration (i.e., the annotations of a program unit and its body are additive).

For context annotations of subunits see 10.2.

If a context annotation consists just of the reserved word **limited** no outside variables that are visible at that point may occur in its scope.

*Examples of context annotations:*

```
     A, B, C : T;

--|  limited to A;
     package P is
         ...   --  A may occur here.
     end P;

     D : T;

     package body P is
         ...   --  A and D may occur here.
     end P;

--|  limited to SIZE;          --   No global variables except SIZE may be used in this body.
     package body QUEUE is

         type TABLE is array (NATURAL range <>) of ITEM;

         STORE      : TABLE(0 .. SIZE - 1);
         COUNT      : NATURAL range 0 .. SIZE := 0;
         IN_INDEX   : NATURAL range 0 .. SIZE - 1 := 0;
         OUT_INDEX  : NATURAL range 0 .. SIZE - 1 := 0;

--|      limited to COUNT;
         function EMPTY return BOOLEAN is
         begin
             return COUNT = 0;
         end EMPTY;
         ...
     end QUEUE;
```

*Note:*

The meaning of a context annotation of a subprogram is similar to declaring the mentioned global variables as *additional* formal in out parameters of the subprogram.


## 10.2 ANNOTATIONS OF SUBUNITS

```
subunit ::=
    separate (parent_unit_name) [context_annotation] proper_body
```

A context annotation of a subunit constrains the use within the subunit of variables from the context of the corresponding body stub, in the same way as a declarative context annotation preceding a body (see 10.1.3).

*Example:*

```
        separate (QUEUE)
--|     limited to STORE, COUNT, IN_INDEX;
        procedure ADD(X : ITEM) is
        begin
            if COUNT < SIZE then
                STORE(IN_INDEX) := X;
                IN_INDEX := (IN_INDEX + 1) mod SIZE;
                COUNT := COUNT + 1;
            else
                raise OVERFLOW;
            end if;
        end ADD;
```


10.3 - 10.6                    No additions

# 11. EXCEPTION ANNOTATIONS

Exceptional behavior may be annotated by annotations of exception handlers, annotations of raise statements, and propagation annotations. The purpose of these annotations is to specify conditions under which a handler expects an exception, conditions under which an exception is raised locally, or conditions under which a subprogram propagates an exception. If the annotations are sufficiently complete, it is possible to prove consistency between programs and annotations in the presence of exceptional behavior (see [14]).

## 11.1          No additions

## 11.2 ANNOTATION OF EXCEPTION HANDLERS

Exception handlers may be annotated exactly as any other sequence of statements. Most important, an annotation at the beginning of the sequence of statements of an exception handler must be true before the handler is executed. Such an annotation therefore constrains the states in which the exceptions that are handled by that handler may be propagated.

*Example of an annotation of an exception handler:*

```
    begin
        ...                              --   sequence of statements
    exception
        when SINGULAR =>
--|         DET(A) = 0;                  --   initial condition for handler
            PUT("A IS SINGULAR");
        when others =>
            PUT("FATAL ERROR");
            raise ERROR;
    end;
```

*Note:*

An annotation at the beginning of a sequence of statements (in particular at the beginning of a handler) is an annotation of a null statement and constrains the initial state whenever that sequence of statements is executed (see 5.1).

## 11.3 ANNOTATION OF RAISE STATEMENTS

Annotations of a **raise** statement are simple statement annotations that constrain the states in which the exception is raised. Generally, assertions are placed immediately *before* a **raise** statement to constrain the states in which the **raise** statement is executed.

Since there is no change of state resulting from a raise statement, unmodified variables in an annotation have the same meaning as if they were modified by **in**.

*Example of an annotation of a **raise** statement:*

```
--|  for all I :  INDEX_RANGE => A(I) ≠ KEY;
      raise NOT_FOUND;
--    NOT_FOUND is raised if KEY is not a component of A.
```

*Note:*

An assertion following a **raise** statement is trivially consistent with the Ada text since it constrains the state of the computation when control reaches its position — a state that is never reached.


## 11.4 PROPAGATION ANNOTATIONS

Propagation annotations are a special kind of annotation for specifying exception propagation. They are basic annotations that may appear as subprogram annotations, statement annotations and declarative annotations.

```
propagation_annotation ::=
    strong_propagation_annotation
  | weak_propagation_annotation

strong_propagation_annotation ::=
    boolean_compound_expression => raise exception_name

weak_propagation_annotation ::=
    raise exception_choice {| exception_choice}
        [=> boolean_compound_expression]
```

A propagation annotation for a subprogram annotates the subprogram specification (see 6.1).

A *strong propagation annotation* of a subprogram specifies a condition on the **in** values of parameters (and global variables) of a call under which an exception must be propagated by the subprogram; the condition need not be true after propagation. The modifier **in** is the default for all constituent variables of the compound expression, i.e. all constituent variables are treated as modified by **in**.

A *weak propagation annotation* of a subprogram specifies exceptions that may be raised as the result of a call to that subprogram, and a condition that will be satisfied by the state of the calling environment when one of those exceptions is propagated. That is, the boolean expression subsequent to => will be true of the computation state of the calling environment at the point when the execution of the subprogram body is abandoned (see [Ada83, 11.4.1]).

A strong propagation annotation of a statement specifies a condition on the initial state under which the statement must raise the exception specified. A weak propagation annotation of a statement specifies exceptions that may be raised by the statement and a condition that must then be satisfied by the computation state at that point, that is when the exception is propagated.

A propagation annotation in a declarative part specifies the propagation of exceptions from the enclosing block or unit resulting from computation within the scope of that annotation; that is, the annotation applies to the elaboration of any subsequent declarations and execution of the constituent statements. The semantics of (weak and strong) declarative propagation annotations are defined analogously to statement propagation annotations.

*Examples of propagation annotations:*

```
    procedure BINARY_SEARCH(A          : in ARRAY_OF_INTEGER;
                            KEY        : in INTEGER;
                            POSITION : out INTEGER );
--|     where ORDERED (A),                      -- an in annotation
--|        out (A(POSITION) = KEY),
--|        raise NOT_FOUND => for all I in A'RANGE => KEY ≠ A(I);
--      A weak annotation: whenever A is ordered and NOT_FOUND is propagated,
--      KEY is not a component of A. This could also be made a strong annotation.

    procedure PUSH(E : in ITEM);
--|     where in STACK.LENGTH = SIZE => raise OVERFLOW,
--|        raise OVERFLOW => STACK = in STACK;
--      A combination of both weak and strong propagation annotations: whenever the stack
--      length is equal to SIZE, a call to PUSH must propagate OVERFLOW;
--      whenever OVERFLOW is propagated the stack state will be equal to its in state.

    X := Y div Z;       --| raise NUMERIC_ERROR => Z = 0 and X = in X;
```

*Notes:*

There may be several propagation annotations for a subprogram or statement, one for each set of exception choices. Because of their textual position, propagation annotations on subprograms and statements cannot refer to variables local to a subprogram body or compound statement.

Weak propagation annotations are analogous to out annotations (assertions) except that they refer to states resulting from propagation of exceptions instead of states resulting from normal termination. Thus, a weak propagation annotation of a subprogram specification acts as a *promise* for each call, specifying a property of the state after the call has resulted in an exception propagation; it also acts as a *constraint* on the body of the subprogram, constraining all states in which an exception may be propagated.

If two or more strong propagation anotations apply to the same unit, their boolean conditions should be mutually exclusive. Otherwise the annotations may specify *simultaneous* propagation of different exceptions, and thereby be inconsistent with the Ada text.

**11.5 - 11.6**          No additions

## 11.7 SUPPRESSING CHECKS OF ANNOTATIONS

The presence of a SUPPRESS pragma in virtual Ada text gives permission to an implementation of Anna by consistency checking (see 1.4) to omit certain runtime checks, as described below.

All checks correspond to situations in which the exception ANNA_ERROR may be raised.

ANNA_CHECK          Check consistency of annotations. If suppressed, an annotation (that refers to the given name, if any) may be considered to hold.

DEFINED_CHECK          Check whether an object V has an initial value. If suppressed, the attribute V'DEFINED may be considered to be TRUE.

QUANTIFIER_CHECK Check a quantified expression (see 4.11). If suppressed, any quantified expression may be considered to be TRUE.

RAISE_CHECK          Check whether for strong propagation annotations, the exceptions are raised under the condition, and, for weak propagation annotations, whether the conditions hold when the exceptions are propagated. If suppressed, the exceptions may still be raised, but strong annotations may be considered omitted, and the condition in weak annotations may be considered to be TRUE.

RESULT_CHECK          Check whether result annotations hold. If suppressed, any result annotation (of the named subprogram) may be considered to hold.

# 12. ANNOTATION OF GENERIC UNITS

Annotations of generic units provide two additional capabilities beyond those provided by annotations of non-generic units: they may be used to constrain actual generic parameters in instantiations, and to express templates for annotations of each instance of a generic unit.

## 12.1 ANNOTATIONS OF GENERIC DECLARATIONS

```
generic_parameter_declaration ::=
    ... ada_generic_parameter_declaration ...
  | generic_parameter_annotation

generic_parameter_annotation ::=
    object_annotation {, object_annotation};
```

A generic parameter annotation is an annotation in the generic formal part. A generic parameter annotation must be an object annotation; it may not contain the modifier out. All program variables occurring in the annotation, including generic formal objects, are assumed to be modified by in by default (similar to subtype annotations and axiomatic annotations). The modifier in refers to the state when the unit is instantiated (and therefore to the value of the actual parameter in that state).

The scope of a generic parameter annotation of a generic declaration is the same as that of a generic parameter declaration at that point.

Generic parameter annotations are elaborated as part of the elaboration of an instantiation of the generic unit. They constrain the actual generic parameters when the generic unit is instantiated: they are evaluated and must be true on instantiation of the generic unit (see also 12.1.1 — 12.1.3 and 12.3). Their truth may then be assumed in the generic unit (see 12.5); if an annotation refers to a generic formal object of mode in out, in can be assumed only for its initial value. Thus, generic parameter annotations are analogous to in annotations on formal parameters of subprograms, where generic instantiation is taken as the analogy to subprogram call.

Annotations appearing in the specification or body parts of a generic unit are called *generic annotations*. They may refer to the generic formal parameters of the unit. Generic annotations are templates that are instantiated together with the Ada text of the generic unit (see 12.3), following the Ada rules for instantiation. Each instance of a generic unit is then annotated by a corresponding instance of the generic annotation.

*Example of a generic annotation of a generic subprogram declaration:*

```
generic
    type ITEM is private;
    with function "*" (U, V : ITEM) return ITEM is <>;
function SQUARING(X : ITEM) return ITEM;
--|      where return X * X;
--       The generic formal subprogram "*" occurs in the annotation; the generic
--       annotation is a template for an annotation of each instance of SQUARING.
```

*Examples of annotations of generic formal parameters and of generic annotations:*

```
      generic
          SIZE : INTEGER;      --| SIZE > 0;
--        An annotation of the generic parameter SIZE that constrains its actual value
--        in any instantiation.
      package DATA is
          BOUND : INTEGER;     --| 0 < BOUND < INTEGER'LAST mod SIZE;
              . . .
      end DATA;
--    The constraint on BOUND is generic; in any instance of DATA it is instantiated by
--    the actual value of SIZE; all values of BOUND must obey the actual constraint.

      generic
          type ITEM is private;
          ZERO : in ITEM;
          with function "+" (X, Y : ITEM) return ITEM is <>;
--|       for all U, V, W : ITEM =>
--|           ZERO + V    = V,
--|           U + ZERO    = U,
--|           (U + V) + W = U + (V + W);
--        The actual "+" operator and ZERO are constrained by this annotation; see 12.1.3.
          type VECTOR is array (POSITIVE range <> ) of ITEM;

      package VECTOR_OPERATIONS is
          LENGTH_ERROR : exception;
          function SUM(A, B : VECTOR) return VECTOR;
--|           where
--|             return C : VECTOR =>
--|                 for all I : INTEGER range A'RANGE => C(I) = A(I) + B(I),
--|             A'LENGTH = 0 or A'LENGTH ≠ B'LENGTH =>
--|                 raise LENGTH_ERROR;

          function SIGMA(A : VECTOR) return ITEM;
              . . .
      end VECTOR_OPERATIONS;


      generic
          type ITEM is private;
          MAXSTACK : NATURAL; --| MAXSTACK > 0;
      package STACK is

--:       function LENGTH return NATURAL;
--:       function "=" (S, T : STACK'TYPE) return BOOLEAN;

          procedure PUSH(X : in ITEM);
--|           where in STACK.LENGTH < MAXSTACK;

          procedure POP(E : out ITEM);
--|           where in STACK.LENGTH > 0;
```

```
--|     axiom
--|       for all ST : STACK'TYPE; X, Y : ITEM =>
--|           ST[PUSH(X); POP(Y)] = ST,
--|           ST[PUSH(X)].POP'OUT(E => Y).E = X,
--|           STACK'INITIAL.LENGTH = 0,
--|           ST.LENGTH ≤ MAXSTACK,
--|             ...;
        end STACK;
```

### 12.1.1 Annotation of Generic Formal Objects

Generic formal objects may be annotated in the generic formal part by object annotations. Such annotations constrain the values of the corresponding actual parameters in instantiations of the generic unit.

*Examples of annotations of generic formal objects:*

```
generic
    SIZE  : INTEGER;     --| SIZE > 0;
    BOUND : in out INTEGER;
package DATA2 is
--|     0 < BOUND < SIZE;
    ...
end DATA2;
```

```
--    The annotation of SIZE constrains any generic actual parameter. The annotation of
--    BOUND is a template for an object constraint since BOUND has mode in out; when
--    it is instantiated the actual (constant) value matched to SIZE constrains the values
--    of the actual variable matched to BOUND.
```

*Notes:*

If a generic formal object has mode **in out**, only the value of the corresponding actual object on instantiation of the generic unit is constrained by annotations in the generic formal part. However, such an object can be constrained in the genric unit by placing an object constraint in the specification part or body of the unit (see above example). Thus a generic formal object of mode **in out** is annotated in the generic unit in the same way as an object global to the unit.

An annotation in the generic formal part, which syntactically is an object annotation, may have the effect of constraining generic actual type and subprogram parameters when the unit is instantiated (see 12.1.2, 12.1.3).

### 12.1.2 Annotation of Generic Formal Types

An object annotation in a generic formal part which refers to a generic formal type by means of type attributes may have the effect of constraining the actual type supplied in an instantiation of the generic unit.

*Examples of object annotations that constrain a generic formal type:*

```
    generic
        type ITEM is private;
        MAX_SIZE : INTEGER;    --| MAX_SIZE > 0;

        type ROW is array (POSITIVE range <>) of ITEM;
--|     ROW'LENGTH < MAX_SIZE;
--      The type ROW is constrained to allow only instantiations to arrays
--      of a maximum length, MAX_SIZE.
    package SORT is
           . . .
    end SORT;

    generic
        SIZE : INTEGER;            --| SIZE > 0;
        type INDEX is range <>;    --| INDEX'FIRST + SIZE = INDEX'LAST;
    package SORT2 is

           . . .
    end SORT2;
--  The annotation referring to INDEX has the effect of constraining any actual type.

    generic
        type SQUARE_MATRIX is array (POSITIVE range <>,
                                     POSITIVE range <>) of ITEM;
--|     SQUARE_MATRIX'LENGTH(1) = SQUARE_MATRIX'LENGTH(2);
    package MATRIX_OPS is
           . . .
    end MATRIX_OPS;
--  Any actual type matching SQUARE_MATRIX is constrained to having
--  the same range in both index positions.
```

*Note:*

The kind of generic formal type parameter determines which attributes are available for use in generic parameter annotations.

### 12.1.3 Annotation of Generic Formal Subprograms

Properties of generic formal subprograms that must be satisfied by actual subprograms in instantiations may be expressed by generic parameter annotations.

*Examples of object annotations expressing properties of generic formal subprograms:*

```
    generic
        type ITEM is private;
        with function "<=" (X, Y : ITEM)  return BOOLEAN is <>;
        type INDEX is (<>);
        type ROW is array (INDEX range <>) of ITEM;

--|     for all X, Y, Z : ITEM  =>
--|         X <= X,
```

```
--|          X <= Y and Y <= X → X = Y,
--|          X <= Y and Y <= Z → X <= Z;
--    This object annotation has the effect of constraining the actual subprogram
--    associated in an instantiation with the relational operator "< = ":
--    it is required to be a partial ordering relation.
      package SORTING is
           . . .
      end SORTING;
```

*Note:*

Generic parameter annotations that constrain generic formal subprograms have a semantics similar to that of axiomatic annotations in a package visible part. Note, however, that in comparison with package axioms the roles of "constraint" and "promise" are reversed in relationship to a package: a generic parameter annotation is a promise to the specification part and body of the generic unit (where the subprograms are used) and constrains its instantiation (where the implementations of the subprograms are supplied), whereas an axiomatic annotation constrains the body of a package and is a promise outside.

## 12.2         No additions

## 12.3 INSTANTIATION OF GENERIC ANNOTATIONS

The instantiation of generic annotations follows the Ada rules for instantiation of generic units.

In an instance of a generic unit, each occurrence of the identifier of the generic unit denotes the instance, i.e., the same entity as the identifier given in the generic instantiation. In Anna, this includes occurrences of the identifier of the generic unit in annotations. For instance, if P is a generic package and Q is declared as an instance of P, then all occurrences of P'TYPE in generic annotations denote Q'TYPE.

During elaboration of a generic instantiation, annotations in the generic formal part are elaborated after all generic actual parameters have been matched (in the Ada sense). The annotations are then evaluated and must be true. Generic parameter annotations thus constrain the generic actual parameters in a generic instantiation (see also 12.1).

Any constraint on an actual parameter that has been imposed before a generic instantiation applies to the instance of the generic unit. This means, in general, that a demonstration of consistency of the instance requires additional analysis to show that constraints on the actual parameters hold, even if the generic unit has previously been shown to be consistent (see 12.5).

*Example of instantiation of generic formal parameter annotations:*

```
C : constant INTEGER := N - M;
subtype SMALL is INTEGER range M..N;
   ...
package SMALL_SORT is new SORT2(C, SMALL);
```

```
--   At the time of this instantiation, elaboration of the parameter constraints
--   yields the following boolean expressions that must evaluate to true:
--      C > 0;
--      SMALL'FIRST + C = SMALL'LAST;
```

*Example of an instance of a generic annotation:*

```
package INTEGER_STACK is new STACK(INTEGER, ...);
```

```
--   the visible part of INTEGER_STACK is an instantiation of that of the generic
--   STACK package:
```

```
--: function "=" (S, T : INTEGER_STACK'TYPE) return BOOLEAN;
      ...
--| axiom
--|     for all ST : INTEGER_STACK TYPE; X, Y : INTEGER =>
--|          ST[PUSH(X); POP(Y)] = ST,
--|          ST[PUSH(X)].POP'OUT(E => Y).E = X,
--|          INTEGER_STACK'INITIAL.LENGTH = 0, ...;
```

## 12.4 EXAMPLE OF A GENERIC PACKAGE WITH ANNOTATIONS

*Example of a specification for a generic SORTING package:*

```
generic
    type ITEM is private;
    with function "<=" (X, Y : ITEM) return BOOLEAN is <>;
    type INDEX is (<>);
    type ROW is array (INDEX range <>) of ITEM;
--|     for all X, Y, Z : ITEM  =>
--|          X <= X,
--|          X <= Y and Y <= X → X = Y,
--|          X <= Y and Y <= Z → X <= Z;
--     This annotation constrains the actual parameter matched to ''<=''
--     to partial ordering relations.
```

```
      package SORTING is

--:         function ORDERED(A : ROW) return BOOLEAN;
--|             where
--|                 return for all I, J : INDEX range A'RANGE =>
--|                     I < J → A(I) <= A(J);

--:         function SWAP(A : ROW; I, J : INDEX) return ROW;
--|             where return A[I => A(J); J => A(I)];

--:         function PERMUTATION(A, B : ROW) return BOOLEAN;
--|             where A'LENGTH = B'LENGTH;
--              Further properties of PERMUTATION are given by the axiomatic annotation below.

            procedure SORT(A : in out ROW);
--|             where
--|                 out (ORDERED(A) and PERMUTATION(A, in A));

--|         axiom for all A, B : ROW; I, J : INDEX range A'RANGE =>
--|             PERMUTATION(A, A),
--|             PERMUTATION(A, B) → PERMUTATION(B, A),
--|             PERMUTATION(A, B) and PERMUTATION(B,C) → PERMUTATION(A,C),
--|             PERMUTATION(SWAP(A, I, J), A);

      end SORTING;
```

## 12.5 CONSISTENCY OF GENERIC UNITS

Annotations of a generic unit have a defined meaning in the context of the generic unit in which they appear. The definition of this meaning and the possibility of analyzing the consistency of generic units before instantiation depends on treating Ada generic units not just as templates, but as having a semantics prior to instantiation. Such a semantics is derived from the semantics of non-generic units as follows. An Ada generic unit has the semantics of an identical non-generic specification (obtained by deleting the formal generic part) or body placed in a declarative part following declarations corresponding to the original formal generic parameters. All corresponding declarations introduce the same identifiers as the generic parameter declarations. The declaration corresponding to a generic formal object parameter declaration is the same, augmented by initialization to a symbolic value; for a formal array type or access type, the declaration corresponding to the generic type parameter declaration is the same; for a private or scalar formal type the declaration corresponding to the generic type parameter declaration may be any type or subtype declaration that matches the formal type parameter; the subprogram declaration corresponding to a generic subprogram parameter specification is obtained by omitting the reserved word with and any optional defaults.

This interpretation of the semantics of generic units permits at least partial analysis of consistency of generic units before any instantiation. For such an analysis, the annotations in the generic formal part, which have the effect of constraining instantiation (see 12.1.1, 12.3), can be assumed to be true of the formal parameters (or, in the case of a generic formal object of mode in out, of the initial value). In the consistency analysis, formal object parameters are treated as symbols, i.e., their names are taken as their values. (This entails that consistency analysis by checking is not always possible.)

120

Consistency of a generic unit does not necessarily imply consistency of any instance of such a unit. Since any constraint on an actual parameter that has been imposed before the generic instantiation also applies to the instance of the generic unit (see 12.3), additional analysis is in general required for a demonstration of consistency of each instance.

*Example of a generic instantiation requiring additional consistency analysis:*

```
generic
    SIZE : INTEGER;          --| SIZE > 0;
    type INDEX is range <>;  --| INDEX'FIRST + SIZE = INDEX'LAST;
package SORT2 is

    . . .
end SORT2;

C : constant INTEGER := N - M;

subtype SMALL is INTEGER range M..N;
--|    where X : SMALL => P(X);
    . . .
package SMALL_SORT is new SORT2(C, SMALL);
```

-- *Consistency with the annotation on the type SMALL requires additional analysis*
-- *of the parameter constraints in the package SMALL_SORT.*

# 13. ANNOTATION OF IMPLEMENTATION-DEPENDENT FEATURES

Representation clauses and implementation-dependent features are not part of Ada programs proper. They do not influence Ada semantics. Consequently, they are ignored in Anna. However, the effect of certain implementation-dependent features can be described by annotations.

## 13.1 - 13.7                    No additions

## 13.8 ANNOTATIONS FOR MACHINE CODE INSERTIONS

The body of a subprogram that contains machine code insertions is ignored in Anna. The specification should, however, include a subprogram annotation that describes the effect of the subprogram. It is then treated analogously to a virtual subprogram whose body has not been supplied.

*Example:*

```
    procedure DIV_REM(N, D : INTEGER; Q, R : out INTEGER);
--|     where D ≠ 0,
--|         out (Q = N div D),
--|         out (R = N rem D);
    ...
    procedure DIV_REM(N, D : INTEGER; Q, R : out INTEGER) is
        use MACHINE_CODE;
    begin
        M_CODE'(LDA,   N'ADDRESS);
        M_CODE'(DIVD,  D'ADDRESS);
        M_CODE'(STA,   R'ADDRESS);
        M_CODE'(STQ,   Q'ADDRESS);
    end;
```

*Note:*

It may be possible to demonstrate consistency between the body with machine code insertions and the subprogram annotations for a specific implementation.

## 13.9 ANNOTATIONS OF INTERFACES TO OTHER LANGUAGES

The specification of a subprogram for which the INTERFACE pragma is given is treated analogously to that of a virtual subprogram in Anna whose body has not been supplied.

*Note:*

It may be possible to demonstrate consistency between a subprogram annotation and the body in the other language.

## 13.10 ANNOTATIONS OF UNCHECKED PROGRAMMING

### 13.10.1 Annotations of Unchecked Storage Deallocation

*Note*:

Using annotations on access types and collections, in the case X is not **null** when FREE(X) is called, it may be possible to demonstrate that there can be no more accesses to the object formerly designated by X via a different access object, say Y. (See [Ada83, 13.10.1].)

### 13.10.2 Annotations of Unchecked Type Conversions

*Note.*

For a given implementation, it may be possible to demonstrate that the conversions maintain the properties expected from objects of the target type.

# A. PREDEFINED ANNA ATTRIBUTES

*Attribute of any object X of any type:*

X'DEFINED      is a Boolean valued attribute. For a scalar object, it yields TRUE if X has a value and FALSE otherwise. For an object of composite type, it yields TRUE if C'DEFINED is true for all components C of X, and FALSE otherwise. For an object of an access type, it always returns TRUE. Private (and generic formal) types are treated according to their full (or instantiated) definition. (See 3.3, 3.5, 3.6.2, 3.7.4., 3.8.2.)

*Attribute of any type T:*

T'INITIAL      denotes the initial value given by default to objects of type T. The initial value is the default initial value or default expression as given in the (sub)type definition of T, or **null** for access types. If no default is given (or defined by Ada), the value of the attribute is undefined. (See 3.3.)

*Attributes of any access type T:*

T'COLLECTION         denotes the current state of the collection of objects of type S designated by values of type T. (See 3.8.2.)

T'COLLECTION'INITIAL denotes the initial state of T'COLLECTION after elaboration of the declaration of T, i.e., an empty collection. (See 3.8.2.)

T'COLLECTION'TYPE    denotes the type of states of the collection T'COLLECTION. (See 3.8.2.)

C'NEXT               For a prefix C that denotes a collection state of type T'COLLECTION'TYPE:
                     Yields the next value of type T to be allocated when the collection has state C.

*Attribute of any procedure P:*

P'OUT          denotes a function that for given in values of the parameters of P returns a record whose components are the out values of the in out and out parameters of P. These values can be selected using the names of the formal parameters of P. The formal parameters to P'OUT are the same as those of P, where the modes are replaced by **in**. Those parameters of P that had mode **out** are treated as having default values in P'OUT. (See 6.8.)

*Attribute of any visible subprogram of a package:*

P'NEW_STATE    denotes a function that expresses the transformation of the package state associated with a visible program P (see 7.7); it returns a value of type S'TYPE, where S is the package declaring P. The formal parameters to P'NEW_STATE are the same as those of P, where the modes are replaced by **in**. Out parameters of P are treated as having default values in P'NEW_STATE. If the new state of package S upon normal completion of the call S.P is ST, then the function call, S.P'NEW_STATE, returns the value ST; otherwise it is undefined. (See 6.8.)

*Attributes of any package P:*

P'INITIAL        is the initial value of the state of P after elaboration of the body of P. (See 7.7.2.)

P'TYPE           is the type of the states of P and is called the *state type of* P.  P'TYPE behaves like a private type exported from P, except that equality may be redefined.  Outside of the package body no structure is visible.  Inside the package body P'TYPE is treated as a record whose components are all the local objects, collections, and package states in the declarative region of P. (See 7.7.1.)

P'STATE          is the current value of the state of P. (See 7.7.2.)

# C. PREDEFINED ANNA ENVIRONMENT

Anna includes the following extensions to the Ada package STANDARD.

*Additional exceptions:*

    ANNA_ERROR : exception

# E. ANNA SYNTAX SUMMARY

**3.1**

```
basic_declaration ::=
    ... ada_basic_declaration ...
    | basic_annotation_list
    | axiomatic_annotation
    | state_type_annotation

basic_annotation_list ::=
    basic_annotation {, basic_annotation};

basic_annotation ::=
    object_annotation
    | result_annotation
    | propagation_annotation
```

**3.2**

```
object_annotation ::=
    boolean_compound_expression
    | out boolean_primary
```

**3.3**

```
full_type_declaration ::=
    ... ada_full_type_declaration ...
    [subtype_annotation]

subtype_declaration ::=
    ... ada_subtype_declaration ...
    [subtype_annotation]

subtype_annotation ::=
    where [in out] identifier : type_mark => boolean_compound_expression ;
```

**3.6.4**

```
array_state ::=
    array_name [array_store_operation {; array_store_operation}]

array_store_operation ::=
    expression {, expression} => expression
```

3.7.5

```
    record_state ::=
        record_name [record_store_operation {; record_store_operation}]

    record_store_operation ::=
        component_simple_name => expression
```

3.8.4

```
    collection_state ::=
        collection_name [collection_operation {; collection_operation}]

    collection_operation ::=
        allocator
      | selected_component => expression
      | indexed_component  => expression
```

4.1

```
    name ::=
        :... ada_name ...
      | initial_name
      | state

    state ::=
        array_state
      | record_state
      | collection_state
      | package_state

    selector ::=
        ... ada_selector ...
      | function_call
```

4.4

```
    compound_expression ::=
        expression  [implication_operator expression]
      | quantified_expression

    relation ::=
        ... ada_relation ...
      | simple_expression [not] isin range
      | simple_expression [not] isin type_mark
      | simple_expression [not] isin collection_name
```

```
primary ::=
    ... ada_primary ...
  | conditional_expression
  | initial_expression
  | (compound_expression)
```

4.5

```
implication_operator ::=
    → | ↔
```

4.11

```
quantified_expression ::=
    quantifier domain {; domain} => boolean_compound_expression

domain ::=
    identifier_list : subtype_indication
  | identifier_list : range

quantifier ::=
    [not] for all | [not] exist
```

4.12

```
conditional_expression ::=
    if condition then
        compound_expression
    {elsif condition then
        compound_expression}
    else
        compound_expression
    end if

condition ::=
    boolean_compound_expression
```

4.13

```
initial_name ::=
    in simple_name

initial_expression ::=
    in (compound_expression)
```

**5.1**

```
simple_statement ::=
    ... ada_simple_statement ...
    | basic_annotation_list

compound_statement ::=
    [compound_statement_annotation]
    ... ada_compound_statement ...

compound_statement_annotation ::=
    with
        basic_annotation_list
```

**6.1**

```
subprogram_declaration ::=
    [context_annotation]
    ... ada_subprogram_specification ...;
    [subprogram_annotation]

subprogram_specification ::=
    [context_annotation]
    ... ada_subprogram_specification ...
    [subprogram_annotation]

subprogram_annotation ::=
    where
        basic_annotation_list
```

**6.5**

```
result_annotation ::=
    return [identifier : type_mark =>] compound_expression
```

**7.1**

```
package_specification ::=
    [ context_annotation ]
    ... ada_package_specification ...

package_body ::=
    [ context_annotation ]
    ... ada_package_body ...
```

**7.7.3**

```
package_state ::=
    state_name [function_call {;function_call}]
```

7.7.5

```
state_type_annotation ::=
    subtype_annotation
```

7.8                                      •

```
axiomatic_annotation ::=
    axiom
        [quantifier domain {; domain} =>]
            boolean_compound_expression {, boolean_compound_expression} ;
```

10.1

```
context_clause ::=
    {with_clause {use_clause} [context_annotation]}

context_annotation ::=
    limited [to name {, name};]
```

10.2

```
subunit ::=
    separate (parent_unit_name) [context_annotation] proper_body
```

11.4

```
propagation_annotation ::=
        strong_propagation_annotation
    | weak_propagation_annotation

strong_propagation_annotation ::=
        boolean_compound_expression => raise exception_name

weak_propagation_annotation ::=
        raise exception_choice {| exception_choice}
            [=> boolean_compound_expression]
```

12.1

```
generic_parameter_declaration ::=
        ... ada_generic_parameter_declaration ...
    | generic_parameter_annotation

generic_parameter_annotation ::=
        object_annotation {, object_annotation};
```

# H. EXAMPLES OF ANNA PROGRAMS


## 1. A SYMBOL TABLE PACKAGE

```
    generic
        type TOKEN is private;
        MAX : POSITIVE;
    package SYMTAB is

        OVERFLOW, NOT_FOUND : exception;

--:     function SIZE return NATURAL;
--:     function "=" (SS, TT : SYMTAB'TYPE) return BOOLEAN;

        function IN_BLOCK(S : STRING) return BOOLEAN;

        procedure INSERT(S : STRING; I : TOKEN);
--|         where in SYMTAB.SIZE = MAX => raise OVERFLOW;

        function LOOKUP(S : STRING) return TOKEN;
--|         where raise NOT_FOUND;

        procedure ENTERBLOCK;

        procedure LEAVEBLOCK;

--| axiom for all SS : SYMTAB'TYPE; S, T : STRING; I : TOKEN =>
--|     SYMTAB'INITIAL[LEAVEBLOCK]      = SYMTAB'INITIAL,
--|     SYMTAB'INITIAL.IN_BLOCK(S)      = FALSE,
--|     SS[ENTERBLOCK; LEAVEBLOCK]      = SS,
--|     SS[ENTERBLOCK].IN_BLOCK(S)      = FALSE,
--|     SS[ENTERBLOCK].LOOKUP(S)        = SS.LOOKUP(S),
--|     SS[INSERT(S,I); LEAVEBLOCK]     = SS[LEAVEBLOCK],
--|     SS[INSERT(S,I)].IN_BLOCK(T)     =
--|         if S = T then TRUE else SS.IN_BLOCK(T) end if,
--|     SS[INSERT(S, I)].LOOKUP(T)      =
--|         if S = T then I else SS.LOOKUP(T) end if;

    end SYMTAB;

    package body SYMTAB is

        type ELEM is
            record
                LEVEL  : NATURAL;
                MEMBER : STRING;
                TOK    : TOKEN;
            end record;

        type STORE is array (1 .. MAX) of ELEM;
        subtype INDEX_RANGE is NATURAL range 0 .. MAX;
```

```
        TABLE    : STORE;
        LEXLEVEL : NATURAL := 0;
        INDEX    : INDEX_RANGE := 0;
```

```
--|     where in out S : SYMTAB'TYPE =>
--|         S.LEXLEVEL ≥ S.TABLE(INDEX).LEVEL;
```

```
--:     function SIZE return NATURAL is
--:     begin
--:         return INDEX;
--:     end SIZE;
```

```
--:     function "=" (SS, TT : SYMTAB'TYPE) return BOOLEAN
--|         where return SS.INDEX = TT.INDEX and
--|             (for all I : INTEGER range 1 .. SS.INDEX =>
--|                 SS.TABLE(I) = TT.TABLE(I));
--:     is separate;
```

```
        function IN_BLOCK(S : STRING) return BOOLEAN
--|         where return exist I : INDEX_RANGE range 1 .. INDEX =>
--|             TABLE(I).MEMBER = S and TABLE(I).LEVEL = LEXLEVEL;
        is
        begin
            for I in reverse 1 .. INDEX loop
                if TABLE(I).LEVEL < LEXLEVEL then
                    return FALSE;
                elsif TABLE(I).MEMBER = S then
                    return TRUE;
                end if;
            end loop;
            return FALSE;
        end IN_BLOCK;
```

```
        procedure INSERT(S : STRING; I : TOKEN)
--|         where in SIZE = MAX => raise OVERFLOW;
        is
        begin
            if INDEX = MAX then
                raise OVERFLOW;
            else
                INDEX := INDEX + 1;
                TABLE(INDEX) := ELEM'(LEXLEVEL, S, I);
            end if;
        end INSERT;
```

```
        function LOOKUP(S : STRING) return TOKEN
--|         where
--|             not exist I : INDEX_RANGE range 1 .. INDEX =>
--|                     TABLE(I).MEMBER = S
--|                 => raise NOT_FOUND,
--|             return J : TOKEN =>
--|                 exist I : INDEX_RANGE range 1 .. INDEX =>
--|                     TABLE(I).MEMBER = S and TABLE(I).TOK = J and
--|                     (for all K : INDEX_RANGE range I + 1 .. INDEX =>
--|                         TABLE(K).MEMBER ≠ S);
```

1. A SYMBOL TABLE PACKAGE

```
        is
            I : INDEX_RANGE;
        begin
            for I in reverse 1 .. INDEX loop
                if TABLE(I).MEMBER = S then
                    return TABLE(I).TOK;
                end if;
            end loop;
            raise NOT_FOUND;
        end LOOKUP;

        procedure ENTERBLOCK
--|         where out (LEXLEVEL = in LEXLEVEL + 1);
        is
        begin
            LEXLEVEL := LEXLEVEL + 1;
        end ENTERBLOCK;

        procedure LEAVEBLOCK
--|         where out (TABLE = in TABLE and
--|             (in LEXLEVEL = 0 or
--|             (LEXLEVEL = in LEXLEVEL - 1 and
--|             in TABLE(INDEX).LEVEL < in LEXLEVEL and
--|             (for all I : INDEX_RANGE range INDEX + 1 .. in INDEX =>
--|                 LEXLEVEL < TABLE(I).LEVEL))));
        is
        begin
            if LEXLEVEL > 0 then
                LEXLEVEL := LEXLEVEL - 1;
                while INDEX > 0 and then TABLE(INDEX).LEVEL > LEXLEVEL loop
                    INDEX := INDEX - 1;
                end loop;
            end if;
        end LEAVEBLOCK;

    end SYMTAB;
```

*Note:*

The implicit full declaration of the symbol table state type assumed in Anna (see 7.7.1.) is:

```
--: type SYMTAB'TYPE is
--:     record
--:         TABLE    : STORE;
--:         LEXLEVEL : INTEGER;
--:         INDEX    : INDEX_RANGE;
--:     end record;
```

The constraint on the state type, LEXLEVEL $\geq$ TABLE(INDEX).LEVEL is a constraint on this full definition. It states that on normal termination of every SYMTAB subprogram, the current value of LEXLEVEL is the LEVEL component of the latest entry in the TABLE.

## 2. DIJKSTRA'S DUTCH NATIONAL FLAG PROGRAM

The package CONCEPTS is a virtual generic package defining the annotation concepts PERMUTATION and SWAPPED. It needs to be instantiated for each context (i.e., set of types) in which it is to be used. The virtual package CONCEPTS does not need a body (see 1.2).

```
--: generic
--:      type INDEX is (<>);
--:      type ELEMENT is private;
--:      type GENERIC_ARRAY is array (INDEX) of ELEMENT;
--: package CONCEPTS is

--: function SWAPPED(A : GENERIC_ARRAY; I, J : INDEX) return GENERIC_ARRAY;

--: function PERM(A, B : GENERIC_ARRAY) return BOOLEAN;

--| axiom for all A, B  : GENERIC_ARRAY; I, J : INDEX =>
--|      SWAPPED(A, I, J)(J) = A(I),
--|      SWAPPED(A, I, J)(I) = A(J),
--|      (K ≠ I and K ≠ J → SWAPPED(A, I, J)(K) = A(K)),
--|      PERM(A, A),
--|      (PERM(A, B) → PERM(B, A)),
--|      (PERM(A, B) and PERM(B, C) → PERM(A, C)),
--|      PERM(SWAPPED(A, I, J), A);

--: end CONCEPTS;

    subtype INDEX is INTEGER range 1 .. 30;
    type COLOR is (RED, WHITE, BLUE);
    type COLOR_ARRAY is array (INDEX) of COLOR;

--: package CONCEPT_INSTANCE is new CONCEPTS(INDEX, COLOR, COLOR_ARRAY);
--: use CONCEPT_INSTANCE;

--: function SAME_COLOR(C : COLOR; A : COLOR_ARRAY; I, J : INTEGER)
--:      return BOOLEAN;
--|      where return for all K : range I .. J - 1 => A(K) = C;

    function SWAP(A : COLOR_ARRAY; I, J : INTEGER) return COLOR_ARRAY;
--|      where return SWAPPED(A, I, J);

    procedure DUTCH(A : in out COLOR_ARRAY; I, J : out INTEGER)
--|      where
--|           out PERM (A, in A),
--|           out (1≤I and I≤J and J≤COLOR_ARRAY'LAST and
--|                SAME_COLOR(BLUE,A,1,I) and SAME_COLOR(WHITE,A,I,J) and
--|                SAME_COLOR(RED, A, J, COLOR_ARRAY'LAST + 1));
--       End of Anna procedure specification
      is
--:      N : constant INTEGER := COLOR_ARRAY'LAST;
         K : INTEGER := COLOR_ARRAY'LAST+1;
--|      PERM(A, in A);
--|      1 ≤ I; I ≤ J; J ≤ K; K ≤ N + 1;
```

```
--   A, I, J and K are constrained throughout the body.  See also Note 1.
     begin
         I := 1;
         J := 1;

         loop --| SAME_COLOR(BLUE,A,1,I) and SAME_COLOR(WHITE,A,I,J) and
              --| SAME_COLOR(RED, A, K, N + 1);                  -- see Note 2
             exit when J >= K;
             if A(J) = BLUE then
                 A := SWAP(A, I, J);
                 J := J + 1;
                 I := I + 1;
             elsif A(J) = WHITE then
                 J := J + 1;
             else   --   A(J) = RED, — see Note 3
                 K := K - 1;
                 A := SWAP(A, J, K);
             end if;
         end loop;
     end DUTCH;
```

Notes:

1. The semicolons separating the inequalities acts like an **and**, except that the inequalities are prefixed individually so that they must be true as soon as their constituent variables have defined values.

2. This assertion has the same semantics as a loop invariant in Hoare's sense.

3. This is an informal comment, but it could be written as an annotation.

4. Each annotation in the body of the procedure DUTCH appears at the place where its scope is largest. These annotations are sufficient to prove the **out** specification of the procedure.

5. Alternative definitions:

```
--    SAME_COLOR could be defined recursively as follows:
--: function SAME_COLOR (C      : COLOR;
--:                       A      : COLOR_ARRAY;
--:                       I, J   : INTEGER)
--:      return BOOLEAN is
--: begin
--:      if I >= J then return TRUE
--:      else
--:          return (A(J - 1) = C and SAME_COLOR(C, A, I, J - 1)) or
--:                 (A(I)     = C and SAME_COLOR(C, A, I + 1, J))
--:      end if;
--: end;
```

```
--    SWAPPED could be defined as:
--|  SWAPPED(A, I, J) (K) =
--|      if K = I then A(J)
--|      elsif K = J then A(I)
--|      else A(K) end if;
```

# REFERENCES

[1]    *The Ada Programming Language Reference Manual*
       US Department of Defense, US Government Printing Office, 1983.
       ANSI/MILSTD 1815A Document.

[2]    Bauer, F.L., Broy, M., Gnatz, R., Hesse, W., Krieg-Brueckner, B., Partsch, P., Pepper, P., and
       Woessner, H.
       Towards a Wide Spectrum Language to Support Program Specification and Program
          Development.
       *ACM SIGPLAN Notices* 13(12):15-24, 1978.
       Also in : Bauer, F.L., Broy, M.(eds); Program Construction. Lecture Notes in Computer Science
          69. Berlin-Heidelberg-New York; Springer 1979. p. 273-289.

[3]    Broy, M., Krieg-Brueckner, B.
       Derivation of Invariant Assertions During Program Development by Transformation.
       *ACM Transactions on Programming Languages and Systems* 2:321-337, 1980.

[4]    Dahl, O.J.
       *Can Program Proving be Made Practical?.*
       Institute of Informatics, University of Oslo, May, 1978.

[5]    Guttag, J.V.
       Abstract Data Types and the Development of Data Structures.
       *Communications of the ACM* 6(20):396-404, June, 1977.

[6]    Guttag, J.V., Horowitz, E., and Musser, D.R.
       Abstract Data Types and Software Validation.
       *Communications of the ACM* 21(12):1048-1063, December, 1978.

[7]    Hoare, C.A.R.
       An Axiomatic Basis for Computer Programming.
       *Communications of the ACM* 12(10):576-581, October, 1969.

[8]    Hoare, C.A.R.
       Proof of Correctness of Data Representations.
       *Acta Informatica* (4):271-281, 1972.

[9]    Hoare, C.A.R.
       Monitors:  An Operating System Structuring Concept.
       *Communications of the ACM* 2(18), 1975.

[10]   Hoare, C.A.R. and Wirth, N.
       An Axiomatic Definition of the Programming Language Pascal.
       *Acta Informatica* 2:335-355, 1973.

[11]   Ichbiah, J.D., Krieg-Brueckner, B., Wichmann, B.A., Ledgard, H.F., Heliard, J.-C., Abrial, J.-R.,
       Barnes, J.P.G., Woodger, M., Roubine, O., Hilfinger, P.N., Firth, R.
       *Reference Manual for the Ada Programming Language: Proposed Standard Document.*
       US Department of Defense, US Government Printing Office, 1980.

[12]     Krieg-Brueckner, B., and Luckham, D.C.
         Anna: Towards a Language for Annotating Ada Programs.
         *Proceedings of the ACM SIGPLAN Symposium on the Ada Programming Language*
              15(11):128-138, December, 1980.

[13]     Luckham, D.C. and Polak, W.
         A Practical Method of Documenting and Verifying Ada Programs with Packages.
         In *Proceedings of the Symposium on the Ada Programming Language*. ACM, November,
              1980.
         ACM SIGPLAN Notices 15(11):113-122.

[14]     Luckham, D.C. and Polak, W.
         Ada Exception Handling: An Axiomatic Approach.
         *ACM Transactions on Programming Languages and Systems* 2(2):225-233, April, 1980.

[15]     Luckham, D.C. and Suzuki, N.
         Verification of Array, Record and Pointer Operations in Pascal.
         *ACM Transacations on Programming Languages and Systems* 1(2):226-244, October, 1979.

[16]     Parnas, D., and Bartussek, W.
         *Using Traces to Write Abstract Specifications for Software Packages.*
         Technical Report UNC Report TR77-012, University of North Carolina, December, 1977.

[17]     Luckham, D.C., German, S.M., vonHenke, F.W., Karp, R.A., Milne, P.W., Oppen, D.C., Polak,
         W., and Scherlis, W.L.
         *Stanford Pascal Verifier User Manual.*
         Technical Report Program Verification Report PV-11, CSD Report STAN-CS-79-731, Stanford
              University, March, 1979.

[18]     Sankar, S. and Rosenblum, D.S.
         *The Complete Transformation Methodology for Sequential Runtime Checking of an Anna
              Subset.*
         Technical Report CSL-TR-86-301, Stanford University, June, 1986.
         Program Analysis & Verification Group Report 30.

# INDEX

This series reports new developments in computer science research and teaching – quickly, informally and at a high level. The type of material considered for publication includes preliminary drafts of original papers and monographs, technical reports of high quality and broad interest, advanced level lectures, reports of meetings, provided they are of exceptional interest and focused on a single topic. The timeliness of a manuscript is more important than its form which may be unfinished or tentative. If possible, a subject index should be included. Publication of Lecture Notes is intended as a service to the international computer science community, in that a commercial publisher, Springer-Verlag, can offer a wide distribution of documents which would otherwise have a restricted readership. Once published and copyrighted, they can be documented in the scientific literature.

**Manuscripts**

Manuscripts should be no less than 100 and preferably no more than 500 pages in length.
They are reproduced by a photographic process and therefore must be typed with extreme care. Symbols not on the typewriter should be inserted by hand in indelible black ink. Corrections to the typescript should be made by pasting in the new text or painting out errors with white correction fluid. Authors receive 75 free copies and are free to use the material in other publications. The typescript is reduced slightly in size during reproduction; best results will not be obtained unless the text on any one page is kept within the overall limit of 18 x 26.5 cm (7 x 10½ inches). On request, the publisher will supply special paper with the typing area outlined.
Manuscripts should be sent to Prof. G. Goos, GMD Forschungsstelle an der Universität Karlsruhe, Haid- und Neu Str. 7, 7500 Karlsruhe 1, Germany, Prof. J. Hartmanis, Cornell University, Dept. of Computer-Science, Ithaca, NY/USA 14850, or directly to Springer-Verlag Heidelberg.

Springer-Verlag, Heidelberger Platz 3, D-1000 Berlin 33
Springer-Verlag, Tiergartenstraße 17, D-6900 Heidelberg 1
Springer-Verlag, 175 Fifth Avenue, New York, NY 10010/USA
Springer-Verlag, 37-3, Hongo 3-chome, Bunkyo-ku, Tokyo 113, Japan

ISBN 3-540-17980-1
ISBN 0-387-17980-1